BIRD

SPAIN

POCKET PHOTO GUIDES

James Lowen & Carlos Bocos

H E L M

LONDON • OXFORD • NEW YORK • NEW DELHI • SYDNEY

HELM
Bloomsbury Publishing Plc
50 Bedford Square, London, WC1B 3DP, UK

BLOOMSBURY, HELM and the HELM logo are trademarks of
Bloomsbury Publishing Plc

First published in the United Kingdom, 2019

A catalogue record for this book is available from the British Library

Library of Congress Cataloguing-in-Publication data has been applied for

ISBN: PB: 978-1-4729-4927-1; eBook: 978-1-4729-4928-8

2 4 6 8 10 9 7 5 3 1

Design by Susan McIntyre
Printed and bound in China by C&C Offset Printing Co.,Ltd

To find out more about our authors and books visit www.bloomsbury.com
and sign up for our newsletters

CONTENTS

INTRODUCTION

Millions of British tourists visit Spain every year – more than any other country, in fact, and not far off the combined total of visitors to France and Germany. While the majority may prioritise their time on sun-drenched beaches, an ever-increasing proportion is exploring Spain's wilder side – especially the birdlife of its remarkably varied countryside.

And for good reason. Spain is the second-largest country to lie wholly within Europe, and boasts a hugely diverse landscape. It has snow-capped mountains that stretch 3km into the sky, where vultures soar around lofty peaks, and swathes of *dehesa* wooded pasture, beneath which Common Cranes nibble acorns each winter. Despite the best (i.e. deleterious) efforts of agricultural intensification, extensive areas remain shrouded in semi-natural grasslands – the steppe-like home of bustards and sandgrouse. There are rocky deserts, a vast central plateau, rich and verdant wetland deltas, ancient oak forests, both Atlantic and Mediterranean coastlines, and the insular havens of the Balearics. And if that were not world enough, Spain lies at the interface between Europe and Africa, funnelling avian migrants between the two continents. It is truly a land of avian plenty.

Moreover, Spain's average human population density of 92 people per km^2 places the country firmly in the more sparsely populated half of the European league table. The UK, by comparison, is roughly three times more densely populated. Furthermore, 80 per cent of Spaniards live in urban areas – which leaves vast areas of uninhabited countryside to explore.

It seems all the more bizarre, therefore, that until now there has never been an English-language field guide focusing on Spain's most common birds. Or indeed – given the boom in digital photography this century – any kind of photographic guide to its avian inhabitants. This book aims to make amends, illustrating and describing 252 bird species that are most likely to be encountered on a visit to Spain, including the Balearic Islands (but excluding the far-flung archipelago of the Canary Islands).

The guide is designed for English-speaking tourists visiting Spain or expats resident in the country who have an interest in identifying birds they see. It aims to meet the needs of ecotourists and novice birdwatchers more than expert birders – although the latter should still get plenty of use from it. This is deliberately a pocket guide, compact enough to carry around and perfect to throw in a suitcase for a family holiday where birdwatching is a sideline.

The book seeks to home in on birds most likely to be seen while exploring the countryside (or urban areas, for that matter; birds get everywhere!) of mainland Spain and the Balearics. Importantly, it seeks to avoid the use of birding jargon, instead conveying in layman's language the features you should look for to identify correctly the bird in your sights.

HOW TO USE THIS BOOK

This book describes and depicts the 252 species you are most likely to see in Spain. Where it makes sense to do so, images of flying birds are included for species often seen in flight.

Each species is introduced by its English and scientific names, plus the total body length (and wingspan for birds frequently seen in flight). The names used, taxonomy (the arbitration on what constitutes a full species rather than subspecies) and the order of families all follow the expert advice of the Association of European Records and Rarities Committees (www.aerc.eu). On pp. 138–142, there is a section on Spanish (Castilian) names, which may be useful if you chat to local birdwatchers. (Note, however, that we don't list Galician, Basque and Catalan bird names, which are in common use in the respective areas.)

Each species description starts with a summary of the distribution, status, seasonality and habitat of the bird in question. This helps start the identification process: you are unlikely to see a summer visitor in winter, or to encounter in Andalucía a bird that occurs only in the Pyrenees. If you are unfamiliar with the geography of Spain, bookmark the map on p. 9, which illustrates the country's administrative regions. (Note, we have used the local names for regions, rather than the English names.)

The text suggests the best ways to distinguish the bird concerned from similar-looking species. Quite intentionally, we neither provide a feather-by-feather description nor recount what you can see in the photographs. Instead, we adopt a more user-friendly approach that directs your attention to the diagnostic characteristics of the species. For example, if Bird A differs from all similar-looking species by having a bold white band on the wing, this is noted but not the colours and patterns of every other feather tract, which in any case will be visible in the accompanying photograph(s). Finally, where relevant to identification (or to getting the jizz, or 'feel', of a bird), we include choice details on vocalisations (such as distinctive calls) and behaviour (showy or skulking, solitary or gregarious). Note that where comparison species are mentioned in accounts, those with their own separate entries are referred to by common name only, whereas species not covered elsewhere in the book are referred to by both their common and scientific names.

HOW TO IDENTIFY A BIRD

To help you identify an unfamiliar bird, it is useful to have a mental checklist of things to look out for. Putting these together should narrow down the list of candidate species. Things to focus on include:

- How does the bird's size compare to a species with which you are familiar (and which, ideally, is nearby)? Is it bigger or smaller?

- How does the shape compare? Is it longer- or shorter-legged? Does it have a long, fine bill or a short, chunky one?

- Where is the bird? Is it in a tree, on the ground, on the water or on a muddy estuary? You are unlikely to see a wader perched in a leafy canopy, or a thrush hopping around on a mudflat.

- What is the bird doing? Specifically, how is it moving? Is it running or hopping? Is it moving quickly through vegetation or flying high in the sky?

- Is the bird silent or vocal? If vocal, can you describe its call or song?

- Are there any obvious patches of white on the bird's plumage? If so, where exactly (see the bird topography illustration below)?

- Finally, look for prominent patches of other colours: perhaps a black stripe on the head, a yellow flash on the wing, or red legs. Where is this and why is it noticeable?

Zoologists pride themselves on being very precise when it comes to describing animals. Ornithologists are no different, and have developed detailed topographic charts to ensure everyone is clear on what parts of a bird they are referring to. This is important when distinguishing between similar-looking species, for example.

However, for the lay reader, and even for many birdwatchers, the particular terms used can be confusing and difficult to remember. Although most people will be able to guess where on a bird's body its rump lies, pinpointing the primaries and supercilium may be trickier. Accordingly, we take care to minimise the use of overly technical terms when referring to parts of a bird's body. For the ease of reading, we simplify descriptions. For example, instead of 'supercilium' we refer to the 'stripe over the eye', and we use 'wing-tip' instead of 'primaries'.

All this said, there is merit in familiarising yourself with the formal terms. It may be useful, for example, in conversations with other birdwatchers who help you differentiate between a Common Chaffinch and Hawfinch by referring to the colour of their wing-coverts. To help prepare for such scenarios, have a look at the annotated bird topography illustration below, which contains the official names for particular body parts, and at the Glossary on p. 136.

BIRD TOPOGRAPHY

forehead
upper mandible
crown
supercilium
ear-coverts
nape
lower mandible
mantle
chin
throat
breast
back
wing-coverts
tertials
scapulars
rump
uppertail-coverts
flank
tail
belly
vent
tarsus
primaries
undertail-coverts
secondaries

NATURAL SPAIN – AN OVERVIEW

The Iberian Peninsula – comprising Spain and Portugal – is isolated from the rest of Europe by the great mountain range of the Pyrenees. The remainder of the landmass is fringed either by the Mediterranean Basin or by the Atlantic Ocean. The coast is important in Spain; only five European countries have a seaboard longer than its 5,000km or so. Nor should Spain's proximity to Africa be underestimated: at its closest point, it is nearer to Morocco than England is to France. Where not overlain with concrete, Spain's Mediterranean coast holds impressive wetlands, jagged cliffs and vast sandy strands. The Atlantic coast tends to be rockier, but is interspersed with estuaries and cosy coves.

Much of inland Spain comprises a vast upland plateau known as the Meseta. One-sixth of Spain lies above 1,000m and, across Europe, only Switzerland has a higher average land height. The Meseta is split by the Sistema Central, a mountain range that peaks just shy of 2,600m. Further north, the Cordillera Cantábrica attains roughly the same altitude in the Picos de Europa. The 400km-long Pyrenees tower above them all, however, reaching 3,400m. The zone above the treeline teems with specialised wildlife, from arctic–alpine plants to hardy butterflies, evolutionarily adapted mountaineering mammals, reptiles and amphibians, and exciting specialist birds such as Bearded Vulture, Wallcreeper, Alpine Chough and White-winged Snowfinch.

As the Meseta tilts towards the south-west, four main rivers (the Duero, Guadalquivir, Guadiana and Tajo) drain into the Atlantic, leaving only the Ebro to exit at the Mediterranean. The Meseta is splattered with rocky gorges and standing waterbodies (particularly reservoirs), which serve as oases for birds – particularly ducks – in an otherwise largely arid, agricultural domain. This is the home of Spain's dwindling 'pseudo-steppes', semi-natural grasslands where Eurasian Stone-curlews rub shoulders with bustards, while various species of lark sing overhead in skies through which sandgrouse career.

Among Spain's natural wetlands are the famous river deltas of the Ebro and Guadalquivir (the latter better known as the Coto Doñana). Reedbeds and marshes nudge lagoons and riverine forests, creating a diversity of landscape packed with herons, gallinules and warblers.

Spain offers wooded habitats, too. Cantabrian slopes are cloaked in Sessile Oak (*Quercus petraea*), Downy Birch (*Betula pubescens*) and Beech (*Fagus sylvatica*). The Pyrenees are renowned for ancient forests of pines (*Pinus* spp.) and European Silver Fir (*Abies alba*). Where these upland woodlands have been cleared for agriculture, grassland has developed – notably hay meadows, in which butterflies and orchids thrive.

Further south lies the *dehesa*, the wooded pasture dominated by Cork Oak (*Quercus suber*) and Holm Oak (*Q. ilex*). This region is of huge significance for wildlife, with the oaks' umbrella-shaped canopy providing nesting sites for Cinereous Vulture, Spanish Imperial Eagle, Great Spotted Cuckoo, Azure-winged Magpie and many more species of bird. Finally, on particularly dry or unstable ground that is no longer suitable for agriculture, secondary scrub communities (usually known as maquis or *garrigue*) have developed. Warblers, shrikes and open-country specialists such as Hoopoe thrive here.

BIRDLIFE IN SPAIN

Of more than 550 bird species recorded in Spain, roughly 350 occur regularly in mainland Spain and the Balearics, and more than 240 routinely breed. Many will be familiar to visitors coming from the British Isles. Excitingly, however, others that are rare at best in the UK and Ireland transpire to be common and widespread in Spain, including Cirl Bunting and European Serin.

You will soon notice other differences, too. Long-legged waterbirds such as egrets, herons and spoonbills are more frequently encountered in Spain. Bustards and sandgrouse roam the rolling, grassy plains, and there is a wider variety of woodpeckers. In addition, there is a much broader diversity of birds of prey (including several eagles and vultures), and many more warblers and larks.

Then there are colourful, exotic-looking creatures such as Hoopoe, European Roller, European Bee-eater and Great Spotted Cuckoo. Gulls include unexpected interlopers, notably Audouin's and Slender-billed. High-altitude zones offer special birds – including such evocatively named species as Alpine Accentor and White-winged Snowfinch.

According to current classifications by BirdLife International and the International Union for Conservation of Nature, 17 species regularly occurring in Spain are considered globally threatened (which means they face a very real chance of extinction), with others on the cusp of being so. Balearic Shearwater breeds nowhere else in the world other than the Balearics. Should you wish to see globally threatened birds such as White-headed Duck, Spanish Imperial Eagle or Southern Grey Shrike in Europe, your best bet is to visit Spain – so we indicate the status of such birds in the species accounts. Make no mistake, Spain is special.

WHERE AND WHEN TO WATCH BIRDS IN SPAIN

You can see birds anywhere in Spain, and need make no special trips to enjoy watching attractive species. But one thing is clear: you will not see precisely the same suite of species wherever you travel. The assemblage of birds at any given location depends on habitat, altitude and season. Below is an overview of interesting birds occurring in particular areas. This section is intended to be illustrative, not exhaustive, and is no substitute for detailed insights on particular locations (for further information, see 'Resources', p. 137).

Northern Spain Although often overlooked by visiting birdwatchers, northern Spain nevertheless provides exciting birdwatching opportunities. The mountains of the Pyrenees and Cordillera Cantábrica excel in high-altitude specialities such as Wallcreeper, Alpine Chough and White-winged Snowfinch. The forested hill slopes hold woodpeckers and warblers. In the east, the arid pseudo-steppes of Aragón house Dupont's Lark and sandgrouse. To the west, Galicia is gaining plaudits as an area to find migrant birds.

Eastern Spain The eastern regions of Cataluña, València and Murcia are the places to see spring migrants passing through on their way to

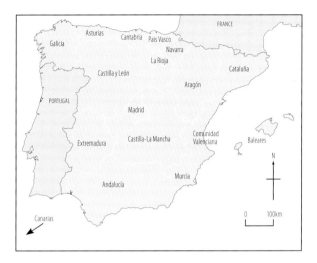

breed further north in Europe. There are also several good wetlands here, most famously the Ebro Delta. This area is renowned for Audouin's and Slender-billed gulls, plus waterbirds from Collared Pratincole and Red-crested Pochard to Purple Swamphen and Glossy Ibis, among numerous egrets, herons and bitterns.

Central Spain This area includes Spain's largest region, Castilla y León, as well as Madrid, Castilla–La Mancha and Extremadura. The first of these is well known for its population of bustards, sandgrouse and Eurasian Stone-curlews, while Castilla–La Mancha has many excellent lagoons and marshes. Extremadura is an outstanding birdwatching destination, with several notable hotspots. The rocky *dehesa* of Monfragüe is brilliant for vultures, eagles and Black Stork. The nearby plains of Cáceres and Trujillo (among others) are good for bustards, larks and sandgrouse, while Trujillo itself is among Spanish towns hosting breeding colonies of White Stork and Lesser Kestrel.

Southern Spain Andalucía largely comprises the archetypal hot Mediterranean landscape. But there are mountains here, too – look for Black Wheatear and Bonelli's Eagle in the Sierra Nevada. In addition, there are wetlands, most famously the Guadalquivir marshes (Coto Doñana), which abound in waterbirds. And there is the Strait of Gibraltar, a honeypot for anyone who enjoys observing migrating birds of prey by the thousand.

The Balearics Nowhere else in Spain better combines birds with beach than Mallorca and its neighbouring islands. Stunning wetlands are complemented by breeding specialities such as Balearic Shearwater, Eleonora's Falcon and Balearic Warbler. It's unmissable!

▲ Adult   ▲ Adults in flight

GREYLAG GOOSE *Anser anser* 80cm

Almost exclusively a winter visitor, with large flocks particularly frequenting wetlands along the river Guadalquivir, lakes in Zamora and Palencia, and parts of Extremadura. Birds occur more widely on passage in October/November and February/March. A few pairs breed. Frequents a variety of waterbodies, pastures and crop fields. The goose species most likely to be seen in Spain. Stocky and thick-necked, it differs from all other geese in its deep-based, wholly orange bill and pink legs. Plumage greyer than other geese, with striking (and unique) pale grey bands on forewings appearing prominent during its ponderous flight. Loud, nasal cackling calls (recalling a 'farmyard goose').

COMMON SHELDUCK *Tadorna tadorna* 60cm

Small, scattered breeding populations, particularly along Mediterranean coasts. Much more common in winter. Particularly favours saltwater habitats, sometimes including saline lakes inland. Unmistakable large, goose-like duck. At a distance, appears white with bold black patches. At closer range, head, neck and inner portion of rear wing have a green sheen, breast-band is chestnut, bill is a vibrant strawberry red and legs are shocking pink. In flight, looks strikingly white, with a dark head, neck, rear third of upper wing, shoulder-patches and upper back. Calls include a nasal, conversational *ga-ga-ga-ga*.

▼ Adult female   ▼ Adult in flight

▲ Adult male

▲ Adult female

MALLARD *Anas platyrhynchos* 55cm

Common countrywide but rare in arid south-east. Resident, but numbers swell in winter. Frequents all types of wetlands, including urban lakes. Familiar long, stocky duck that provides a benchmark for identifying other ducks. In flight, looks heavy and dark, with two white lines along wings flanking a blue rectangle. Orange legs (visible when on land) are unlike those of any other Spanish duck except the massive-billed Northern Shoveler. Male's combination of green head, thin white neck collar, purple-brown breast and curly black tail feathers is unique. Female differs from female Gadwall in its stripier face and limited (rather than extensive) orange sides to grey bill. Beware oddly plumaged birds (black, white, etc.) deriving from captive stock.

EURASIAN WIGEON *Anas penelope* 46cm

Widespread and common winter visitor throughout Spain, especially along the coast. Frequents waterbodies and marshes. Midway between Mallard and Eurasian Teal in size, with a short neck and round head. Bill pattern is unique among European dabbling ducks: pale bluish with a black tip. Male's chestnut head and yellow forehead-stripe are distinctive; in flight, shows a striking white patch on forewing. Female dull brown, differing from other ducks by having subtly chestnut flanks and (visible when on land) a contrasting white belly. Gregarious, sometimes in large groups that utter evocative whistling calls and take to the air in rapid, wheeling flocks.

▼ Adult male

▼ Adult female

▲ Adult male   ▲ Adult female

GADWALL *Anas strepera* 51cm

Resident populations scattered across Spain, particularly in major wetland regions. More widespread in winter. Favours larger, well-vegetated freshwater bodies. Slightly smaller and more slender than Mallard. Male is the only duck with almost wholly silvery-grey plumage and contrasting black bill. In flight, white patch at rear of wing catches one's eye. Female resembles female Mallard but has a plainer face and more extensive orange sides to bill. Usually occurs in pairs; flocks are rare. Rather unobtrusive; rarely vocal.

EURASIAN TEAL *Anas crecca* 36cm

Very rare breeder in a few well-vegetated waterbodies in Galicia and Asturias. Winters commonly, particularly in extensive wetlands, marshes and large estuaries. Spain's smallest dabbling duck, and appears particularly compact in its urgent, twisting flight. Often in dense flocks. Smaller groups are very nervous, fleeing rapidly (and almost vertically) at the slightest sign of danger. Attractive males have a rufous head partitioned by a broad green mask with yellow edges. Grey body is divided by two horizontal stripes (one black, one white), and a yellow triangle on vent glows on gloomy afternoons. Diminutive size distinguishes female from other brown female ducks, e.g. Eurasian Wigeon. Female differs from female Garganey in plainer head, white line along side of tail and (often) orange base to bill.

▼ Adult male   ▼ Adult female

▲ Adult male   ▲ Adult female

NORTHERN PINTAIL   *Anas acuta*   56cm (+ 10cm tail in male)

Rare breeder. Relatively common in winter in coastal wetlands (scarce inland). Both sexes are slender, long-necked, sharp-winged, graceful ducks – the male with elongated tail-streamers. Male is distinctive, with a chocolate-brown head contrasting with white breast, and a cream stripe on rear flanks contrasting with black vent and undertail. Female differs from female Mallard and Gadwall in lacking any orange on bill, and having an entirely plain head and whitish breast. Usually occurs as loose groups in flocks of other ducks.

GARGANEY   *Anas querquedula*   39cm

Localised breeder (summer visitor) in central and southern Spain. More widespread on migration. Shy, preferring secluded, well-vegetated lakes, especially flanked by reeds. Slightly larger than Eurasian Teal, but unlike that species, upends only rarely to feed, preferring to dabble on surface. At a distance, male is a duck of two halves – dark-fronted, but pale at the rear. At closer range, head pattern (long white stripe from eye to nape, on chocolate-brown head) is distinctive. Female and juvenile/first-winter resemble female Eurasian Teal but differ in boldly striped face, contrastingly creamy chin and all-dark bill (Eurasian Teal often has an orange bill base).

▽ Adult male   ▽ Adult female

▲ Adult male

▲ Adult female

NORTHERN SHOVELER *Anas clypeata* 48cm

Rare, localised breeder in major wetlands; more widespread and common in winter. Favours shallow, well-vegetated waterbodies. Smaller, stockier and with a bigger head than Mallard, and with a massive spatulate bill (the origin of its name) that makes identification easy. Male is distinctive, with a green head (like male Mallard) but white breast and rusty flanks. In flight, male has eye-catching large, pale blue upperwing-patch (grey in female). Female recalls female Mallard in plumage, but has a plainer head. Forages undemonstratively, usually in pairs and never in flocks.

RED-CRESTED POCHARD *Netta rufina* 55cm

Sparse, shy breeder of well-vegetated lakes in major wetlands, moving to follow suitable conditions. More widespread in winter, favouring large waterbodies. Notable moulting congregation at Orellana Dam, Extremadura. Large-headed duck, the size of a Mallard, which feeds by dabbling and upending. At a distance, male can look mainly dark and white, but diagnostic burnt orange head and vivid red bill remain highly visible. Female is uniform, unmarked brown but with a contrasting bicoloured head (dark cap, pale cheeks) – a far more striking pattern than superficially similar female Common Scoter. In flight, shows a prominent white wing-stripe.

▼ Adult male

▼ Adult female with duckling

COMMON POCHARD *Aythya ferina* 46cm

Vulnerable. Scarce, local breeder; numbers vary with water levels. Common, widespread winter visitor – often on expansive, sparsely vegetated waterbodies. Diving ducks such as Common Pochard are fairly small – about the size of Eurasian Wigeon – but compact and stocky. They feed by diving fully underwater and are typically gregarious. Both sexes of Common Pochard have a distinctive profile, with a gently sloping forehead and longish bill. Head of male (above) is a deeper chestnut than in male Red-crested Pochard and bill is blue-grey/black (red on latter). Female has a dark eye surrounded by diffuse pale 'spectacles' – quite unlike the staring yellow eye of female Tufted Duck.

TUFTED DUCK *Aythya fuligula* 42cm

A few pairs breed in northern Spain. Scattered winter populations, particularly in Galicia, Asturias, Extremadura and Castilla–La Mancha, when it favours deep water. Marginally smaller and slighter than Common Pochard, with a shorter bill. Female differs from female Common Pochard by having a vibrant yellow eye and pale blue bill with a black tip; it may also have a hint of a tuft on rear crown, which becomes a long crest in male. Latter is unmistakable, being all black with white flanks. In flight, both sexes have a prominent white stripe on rear wing (indistinct in Common Pochard).

▽ *Adult male*

▽ *Adult female*

▲ Adult male   ▲ Adult female

COMMON SCOTER *Melanitta nigra* 49cm

Gregarious seaduck, occurring along Spanish coasts on autumn passage. Common winter visitor on Atlantic coasts; rare in the Mediterranean. Between Eurasian Wigeon and Mallard in size, but stockier. Both sexes are wholly dark (or almost so), males black and females sooty brown, with no white on wing. Female has a pale cheek-patch – more indistinct than in female Red-crested Pochard (and lacking that species' conspicuous white wing-stripe). Typically observed in large groups bobbing on the sea, or flying in long lines low over the water (when seen as chunky, short-necked, all-dark ducks), as if playing follow-my-leader.

WHITE-HEADED DUCK *Oxyura leucocephala* 45cm

Endangered. Scarce resident of scattered, well-vegetated lakes in the south. Unmistakable duck, threatened with global extinction but with its western stronghold in Spain. The size of a Common Pochard, but looks smaller and stockier as length includes its long, pointed tail (often held at 45 degrees to the water). Smaller and rounder than Common Scoter and Red-crested Pochard, females of which recall male White-headed Duck, having a pale face contrasting with black cap. Male White-headed's face is bright white, however, and swollen blue bill and chestnut tones to remaining plumage are distinctive. Female dowdier than male, with broad black cheek-stripe and extensive dark crown interrupting white face; bill is also large but black.

▼ Adult male   ▼ Adult female

COMMON QUAIL *Coturnix coturnix* 17cm

Summer migrant, inhabiting grassy plains, cultivated fields and valleys throughout Spain, except in upland Cantabria. Tiny (the size of a Eurasian Skylark), skulking gamebird that stays hidden in vegetation. Best located by male's song: a far-carrying, liquid, trisyllabic *wit-wi-wit*. Diminutive stature rules out Grey Partridge (*Perdix perdix*; not illustrated, occurs in northern mountains) as a confusion species, although streaky, camouflaged brown plumage is not dissimilar. Also appears much longer-winged than Grey in flight (surprisingly so) and drops into cover on landing. Red-legged Partridge is far too boldly patterned to be a confusion species. Crakes (*Porzana* spp., not illustrated) could also cause confusion, but they inhabit marshes rather than dry grasslands.

RED-LEGGED PARTRIDGE *Alectoris rufa* 34cm

Common resident throughout Spain, mainly below 1,500m. Partridges are fat-bodied, small-headed birds that dot agricultural fields. They are wary, preferring to run when feeling threatened, but may fly low, with rapid wingbeats and stiff-winged glides. Red-legged is more colourful and boldly patterned than Grey Partridge (*Perdix perdix*; not illustrated, occurs in northern mountains), with red (not grey) bill and legs. In flight, shows plain wings (barred in Grey). Much larger than Common Quail. Call often heard: a rhythmic, grating, jerky spluttering. Gregarious outside the breeding season.

GREAT NORTHERN DIVER *Gavia immer* 81cm

Also known as Common Loon. Scarce winter visitor off coasts of north-west Spain (Galicia and Cantabria); rare elsewhere, occurring occasionally on inland reservoirs. Nevertheless, the most likely of Spain's three similarly distributed species of diver to be encountered; the others (not illustrated) are Red-throated (*Gavia stellata*) and Black-throated (*G. arctica*). Great Northern is bigger and stockier than both, with a thicker, dagger-shaped bill, broader neck and more angular head. Take care to avoid confusion with the more common Great Cormorant and European Shag. Unlike those species, Great Northern Diver will never be seen perching upright on land. The diver is also heftier than both (which are rakish in comparison), with deeper, almost goose-like wingbeats during its muscular flight, when its long, trailing feet are obvious.

LITTLE GREBE *Tachybaptus ruficollis* 26cm

Common resident of well-vegetated freshwater bodies throughout Spain, but scarce in mountains. Gregarious in winter. Tiny and rounded: the smallest bird likely to be seen swimming on lakes etc. (much smaller than Eurasian Teal). Shorter-necked and dumpier than other grebes. Markedly fluffy, with a shaggy rear end. The brownest grebe – never strikingly black and white like winter-plumaged Black-necked Grebe, which also has a black bill (yellow in winter-plumaged Little). In summer plumage, adults have a unique chestnut cheek and yellow patch by bill.

▼ *Adult summer* ▼ *Adult winter*

▲ Adult summer ▲ Adult winter

GREAT CRESTED GREBE *Podiceps cristatus* 49cm

Common throughout on sheltered, vegetated waterbodies. More widespread in winter, when seen especially on deep reservoirs. Largest grebe, the size of a Northern Shoveler, but much more rakish. Longer- and thinner-necked than other grebes. In summer plumage, no other grebe has a black crest, white face and white neck. In winter garb, long pink bill and white stripe above dark eye rule out Black-necked Grebe. First two characters plus white (not dusky) neck also eliminate Red-necked Grebe (*Podiceps grisegena*; not illustrated, winters only very rarely in northern Spain).

BLACK-NECKED GREBE *Podiceps nigricollis* 31cm

Frequent winter visitor along the Mediterranean coastline and nearby freshwater lakes. Scattered breeding colonies throughout Spain, but fickle, nesting only where conditions suit. Small size eliminates confusion with Great Crested Grebe. Distinctive in breeding plumage, with a golden fan of feathers behind eye, contrasting with red eye, predominantly black plumage and chestnut flanks. In winter, differs from Little Grebe by having black, white and grey plumage (not brown and beige), and a black bill and red eye (yellow and black, respectively, in Little). More similar to Horned (Slavonian) Grebe (*Podiceps auritus*; not illustrated, scarce winter visitor to Cantabrian coasts), but slightly smaller, with a fluffy 'bottom', slightly upturned bill and steeper forehead (which lend it a different profile), and typically much duskier neck.

CORY'S SHEARWATER *Calonectris diomedea* 53cm, wingspan 113cm

Two very similar-looking subspecies of Cory's Shearwater occur in Spain (and they are sometimes treated as separate species). The one you are most likely to see is Scopoli's Shearwater (subspecies *diomedea*), which is a summer breeder on the Balearic Islands and in a few mainland colonies. It is seen off other coasts on passage (particularly in the Strait of Gibraltar). Cory's Shearwater (subspecies *borealis*) breeds on the Canary Islands and migrates past Atlantic coasts. Both are the size of Lesser Black-backed Gull (therefore much bigger than Balearic Shearwater), but with longer, slimmer wings. They also fly differently to gulls, with lethargic downbeats and long glides on bowed wings. Beware confusion with young Northern Gannet, which is much larger, with angled wings, and a longer bill and tail.

BALEARIC SHEARWATER *Puffinus mauretanicus* 36cm, wingspan 84cm

Critically Endangered. Breeds exclusively in the Balearics (March–June), particularly Formentera. On passage (particularly June–October), seen off all coasts as it wanders to the Bay of Biscay and further north. Winters off north-east Spain (December–January). Smaller seabird than Cory's Shearwater; looks longer-tailed in flight due to projecting toes, and is more compact and distinctly dusky, particularly on head and underparts. Flight is rapid, on quick

wingbeats, and generally low over water. More heavily built and duskier than black-and-white Manx Shearwater (*Puffinus puffinus*; not illustrated, uncommon on Atlantic coasts). Lacks cruciform shape, high/looping glides and silvery underwings of almost blackish Sooty Shearwater (*P. griseus*; not illustrated, common off Atlantic coast).

▲ Adult in flight   ▲ Juvenile in flight

NORTHERN GANNET   *Morus bassanus*   92cm, wingspan 180cm

Passage migrant along Atlantic and Cantabrian coasts, particularly in autumn (August–November), with lower numbers in spring (February–April). Spain's largest seabird, substantially larger than Great Black-backed Gull (*Larus marinus*; not illustrated, scarce winter visitor to coasts), although its elegance belies its size. Flies with deep, airy wingbeats. Catches attention by dramatically plunging into sea when foraging. Unique shape is key to identification of distant birds (particularly youngsters): long wings angled back from 'elbow'; long, slender tail; and elongated head and bill. First-winter brown, gradually whitening with age until reaching adult plumage (all white save for extensive black wing-tips and orange-yellow wash to head) at about four years old.

GREAT CORMORANT   *Phalacrocorax carbo*   85cm

Increasingly common and widespread winter visitor throughout Spain, particularly along coasts and river valleys. Frequents shores and inland freshwaters. Large, long-billed, dark waterbird. Swims low in water with bill tilted upwards. Stands erect, often stretching out wings to dry. Flocks typically fly in 'V' formation like geese, but look broader-winged than latter, with a long, broad tail, and often glide. See European Shag (most likely confusion species) and Great Northern Diver for differences from those species.

EUROPEAN SHAG *Phalacrocorax aristotelis* 73cm

Strictly coastal, breeding on rocky islands and ledges. Winters offshore, including around harbours. Widespread resident along Atlantic, Cantabrian and Balearic shores, with scattered populations elsewhere. Very similar to Great Cormorant but markedly smaller and more slender, with a thin neck. Often dives with a pronounced leap (cormorant tends to roll underwater). Adult European Shag (above) lacks Great Cormorant's white patches on cheek and (in breeding plumage) thigh/head, lacks bronzy sheen on wings, and has a more angular head and a tousled crest. Immature differs from Great Cormorant in more uniform underparts, smaller area of yellow facial skin and white chin.

LITTLE BITTERN *Ixobrychus minutus* 36cm

Uncommon, sparsely distributed breeder in reedbeds and well-vegetated waterbodies, particularly along major river valleys. Summer visitor; rare in winter. Very small heron, size of Common Moorhen. Clandestine, making only short appearances in the open – normally in flight, when it flies rapidly for a short distance on elastic wingbeats. Male distinctively plumaged: black back and crown (shared only with larger Black-crowned Night Heron), but otherwise cream and striped (not grey/white and plain). Bicoloured wings are eye-catching in flight. Female and immature resemble a tiny Eurasian Bittern (*Botaurus stellaris*; not illustrated, rare resident in small pockets across Spain), but buffier, with a streakier back and stripier underparts. Male's call is a gruff bark.

▼ *Adult male*

▼ *Adult female*

▲ Adult ▲ Adult in flight

BLACK-CROWNED NIGHT HERON *Nycticorax nycticorax* 62cm

Uncommon, sparsely distributed breeder in reedbeds and well-vegetated waterbodies, particularly along major river valleys. Mostly a summer visitor; scarce in winter. Prefers marshy vegetation, often by waterbodies, and roosts in trees. Largely nocturnal, typically emerging at dusk, when it flies on easy crow-like wingbeats. Mid-sized heron, but stocky, big-headed and thick-necked. Adult distinctively tricoloured, with large blocks of black, grey and white unfettered by stripes or streaks (unlike, say, the smaller Little Bittern). Immature differs from Eurasian Bittern (*Botaurus stellaris*; not illustrated, rare resident in small pockets across Spain) by being dark brown with whitish droplets across wings and back, and narrow stripes on throat and breast.

SQUACCO HERON *Ardeola ralloides* 45cm

Summer visitor to scattered wetlands, particularly large ones, in southern, central and eastern Spain. Frequents marshes, ditches and damp meadows, usually with scattered bushes and trees. Spain's second-smallest heron and one that is surprisingly camouflaged – until it takes flight, at which point it shocks with egret-like white wings and tail. Confusion with egrets (particularly marginally larger Cattle Egret) is removed, however, by peachy-buff (summer adult) or sandy-brown back and head. At peak of courtship, adults are stunning creatures, with reddish feet, long head plumes and a black-tipped blue bill.

▽ Adult ▽ Adult in flight

CATTLE EGRET *Bubulcus ibis* 48cm

Locally common species, concentrated in the south-west quarter of Spain, along the Mediterranean coast and inland to the Basque Country. Resident, but wanders outside the breeding season. Frequents marshes and damp meadows, often hunting insects flushed (as its name suggests) by cows. Small, compact, thick-necked heron that typically sits hunched. Differs from Squacco Heron in slightly larger size and white back/underparts. Smaller and stockier than Little Egret, with a shorter neck and legs, and a short, pale bill. Great Egret, like Cattle, has a pale bill but is much larger and more slender. In summer, adult has extensive peachy patches on crown, breast and mantle; legs turn pale and bill becomes pinkish red.

From top: adult winter, adult summer

LITTLE EGRET *Egretta garzetta* 60cm

Increasingly common breeder, mainly in south-west Spain. More widespread in winter, particularly along coasts. Frequents marshes, rivers and lakes; also saltpans and shorelines. All-white plumage means the only confusion species are other egrets. In size, nearer Cattle Egret than Great Egret. Closer to the latter in shape (long legs, neck and bill). Bare parts are key to identification: adult Little has a black bill/legs and yellow feet year-round (greener in juvenile); Cattle always has a pale bill/legs; Great has a black bill (but pale legs) in summer and dark legs (but yellow bill) in winter. Motionless for long periods, then suddenly springs into action, running, leaping and making lightning grabs for aquatic prey.

GREAT EGRET *Egretta alba* 95cm

Scarce summer visitor, breeding particularly in the Ebro Delta and Guadalquivir wetlands. Winter birds seen mainly in Cataluña. Favours wetlands, coastal lagoons, saltpans and paddyfields. Very large – the size of a Grey Heron, but looking taller and much slimmer, with a long, slender, serpentine neck. All-white plumage means Cattle Egret and Little Egret are the main confusion species, but much larger than both (for differences in bare-part coloration, see Little). Bigger also than all-white Eurasian Spoonbill, with a shorter, dagger-like (rather than spatulate) bill. At a distance, conceivably confusable with Mute Swan (*Cygnus olor*; not illustrated, rare winter visitor to northern coasts), but has a much longer bill and legs.

GREY HERON *Ardea cinerea* 93cm

Common resident throughout Spain, with population swollen by winter visitors. In the breeding season, most common in the west; in winter, seen along coasts. Frequents all kinds of watercourses and agricultural land, where it feeds on small mammals. Large, long-legged, long-necked and mostly greyish bird. Often motionless – a stealth hunter. Flight is slow on deep wingbeats, with broad wings held at a sharp angle. Lack of brown plumage prevents confusion with Eurasian Bittern

▲ *Adult in flight* ▼ *Adult*

(*Botaurus stellaris*; not illustrated, rare resident in small pockets across Spain) and young Purple Heron. Adult Purple Heron is much more colourful, with rufous, chestnut and mauve swathes, plus thick black stripes on neck-sides. Harder to tell apart in flight, but Purple's wings are tricoloured and less contrasting than Grey's bicoloured wings. Purple's neck 'keel' is also more angular than the rounded equivalent of Grey.

▲ Adult in flight   ▲ Adult

PURPLE HERON   *Ardea purpurea*   80cm

Summer breeder, occasional in winter. Fairly common, particularly in coastal wetlands in the south and east; range is expanding north. More often associated with extensive reedbeds and shallow marshes than larger Grey Heron (for differences, see that species). Colourful adult is distinctive, and – with good views – unlikely to be mistaken for anything else. Juvenile could be confused with Eurasian Bittern (*Botaurus stellaris*; not illustrated, rare resident in small pockets across Spain), having essentially brown plumage, a dark cap, streaked foreneck and striped face. Shape eliminates confusion: Eurasian Bittern is thickset and deep-billed, whereas Purple Heron has a long, tapered, serpentine neck and elongated bill.

BLACK STORK   *Ciconia nigra*   100cm

Largely a summer visitor to the southern half of western Spain. Hunts in small rivers; breeds on cliffs and, occasionally, tall trees. A few winter in southern Spain. Widespread on migration; particularly frequent in the east in autumn. Massive, long-legged bird – larger than Grey Heron. Storks are almost vulture-like in flight – with long, broad wings ending in separated 'fingers' – but long neck/bill and long, trailing legs make for a very different silhouette. Realistically, can be confused only with White Stork, but lankier than that species, with a slimmer neck. Also, plumage is largely black (brown in juvenile) rather than largely white, with white restricted to belly, undertail and 'armpits'.

▼ Adult   ▼ Juvenile in flight

▲ Adult   ▲ Adult in flight

WHITE STORK *Ciconia ciconia* 105cm

Resident population boosted by summer migrants. Common breeder in the western half of Spain, particularly Extremadura and Castilla y León; also seen on migration. Typically occurs in open fields and wet meadows – more open terrain than Black Stork. Builds a huge stick nest in trees or atop buildings. Massive and unmistakable. Differs from other large white birds such as Great Egret and Eurasian Spoonbill by its half-black wings, and bright red bill and legs. To distinguish it from Black Stork, see that species.

GLOSSY IBIS *Plegadis falcinellus* 60cm

Uncommon resident of major wetlands in the east and south (particularly Doñana); more frequent on autumn migration. Extinct in Spain until recently, but has now recolonised. Although herons and egrets are also long-legged, long-necked, long-billed waterbirds, Glossy Ibis is unrelated. It is easily identified by dint of its all-dark plumage and downcurved (rather than straight) bill. In flight, its slim neck strains forward from wings – quite unlike the hunch-necked Eurasian Bittern (*Botaurus stellaris*; not illustrated, rare resident in small pockets across Spain). The decurved bill means the ibis could be confused with the Eurasian Curlew, but it is wholly dark (usually looking black, or glossy maroon in summer adult), lacks curlew's white 'V' on rump, and in flight shows long neck and trailing legs.

▲ Adult in flight | ▲ Adult (left), juvenile (right)

EURASIAN SPOONBILL *Platalea leucorodia* 85cm

Breeds colonially in a few wetlands, mainly on the south-west coast. More visible on spring and autumn migration, when flocks are often seen resting in shallow freshwater bodies. Slightly smaller than Grey Heron. Although wholly white like egrets (albeit with black wing-tips in juvenile), unlikely to be confused unless asleep with unique spatula-shaped bill concealed under its wing. Unlike egrets, flies with neck outstretched – and shape is more reminiscent of swans (*Cygnus* spp.). Smaller than the latter, however, and with more hurried wingbeats and protruding legs.

GREATER FLAMINGO *Phoenicopterus roseus* 120–145cm

Occurs along the Mediterranean and south-western coasts, inhabiting saltpans and shallow saline lakes. Breeding success depends on water levels; most successful colony is in Málaga. Unmistakable shape, combining immensely long legs, very long S-shaped neck and remarkable deep, down-kinked bill. Shape equally striking in hurried, rather mechanical flight, when legs and neck are extended and held rigidly horizontal. Adult very colourful, being pale pink, with deeper pink and extensive black areas on wings (therefore looking tricoloured in flight). Juvenile dowdy, being dirty white with scruffy brown feathering on mantle, and grey legs.

◀ Adult
▼ Adult in flight

EUROPEAN HONEY BUZZARD *Pernis apivorus* 55cm, wingspan 120–150cm

Summer visitor, breeding in northern and central Spain. Uncommon and unobtrusive, favouring large forests near open areas. More common on migration, particularly in funnels such as the Pyrenees and Strait of Gibraltar. Not a true buzzard, but very similar – Common Buzzard is key confusion species. Secretive inside forest, so usually seen in flight. Typically soars with wings held flat (generally raised in a shallow 'V' in Common) and glides with wings held downwards (level in Common). Shape is also subtly different: neck and tail longer, and wings narrower, with straighter rear edge. Plumage variable, but often shows a neat black trailing edge to underwing and a more noticeably banded tail. Unique display flight – performed high above trees – sees male swooping upwards and then fluttering wings above back.

BLACK-WINGED KITE *Elanus caeruleus* 33cm, wingspan 76–88cm

Uncommon resident, with population centred on Extremadura, but expanding. Favours oak forests and cultivation. Unmistakable raptor. Size of a Common Kestrel, but more thickset and with a larger head. In flight, shape is distinctive, with a very short, square-cut tail and broad-based but pointed wings. Pale, ghostly grey plumage means confusion possible only with male Hen or Montagu's harriers. Adult's black 'shoulder pads' and juvenile's extensive black wing-tip distinguish them from both harriers; in addition, all ages have white tail sides, and lack harriers' white rump. Varied flight styles: hovers like Common Kestrel, glides on raised wings, and hunts with deep wingbeats like Short-eared Owl.

▼ Adult in flight

▼ Adult

▲ *Adult*　　　　　　　　　　　　▲ *Adult in flight*

BLACK KITE *Milvus migrans*　53cm, wingspan 135–155cm

Summer visitor throughout most of Spain, with the exception of the Mediterranean coast. Most common in major river valleys. Large, dark raptor, flying with bowed wings, twisting tail and regular swoops. Flight style, gently forked tail and more obviously 'fingered' wing-tip (primaries) should remove confusion with buzzards and harriers, but beware moulting immature or female Western Marsh Harrier, which may have a ragged tail or wings. Look also for Black Kite's distinctive white flash on underside of wing at base of the wing-tip. See Red Kite for differences from that species.

RED KITE *Milvus milvus*　67cm, wingspan 140–165cm

Near Threatened. Resident in a broad swathe of central/western Spain, but absent from the east and north-west. More widespread and common in winter, when population is supplemented by immigrants from further north. Prefers more wooded habitat than Black Kite but routinely hunts in open areas. Distinctive large, fork-tailed bird of prey with long, supple wings; flight agile and swooping, with a twisting tail. Black Kite is only confusion species – and, even then, only between spring and autumn. Best differentiated by narrower wings (five 'fingers' at wing-tip rather than six); longer, more obviously forked and distinctly chestnut tail; more contrasting and colourful plumage; and large white flash on underwing, isolating black wing-tip.

▼ *First-winter*　　　　　　　　　▼ *Adult in flight*

BEARDED VULTURE *Gypaetus barbatus* 115cm, wingspan 235–275cm

Near Threatened; also called Lammergeier. Sparsely distributed resident of mountains in the Pyrenees, with outposts in the Basque mountains and Picos de Europa. Most likely seen patrolling steep slopes, cliffs or high above valleys. Dramatic vulture that feeds by dropping mammal bones from a height to smash them (the Spanish name *Quebrantahuesos* means 'bone-breaker'). Distinctive shape: longer- and slimmer-winged than other vultures, with a diagnostic elongated wedge-shaped tail that is clearly longer than width of wing. Only Egyptian Vulture approaches this shape, but it is barely half the size, with blunter wings and a shorter tail. Juvenile plumage starts dark, then pales with age to become contrastingly peach/black in adults.

EGYPTIAN VULTURE *Neophron percnopterus* 60cm, wingspan 155–170cm

Endangered. Summer migrant to Spain, with four broad breeding areas in mainland Spain (plus one in the Balearics), largely in mountains and rugged gorges. Smallest vulture by a long way, with broad wings and a longish wedge-shaped tail. All-dark juvenile confusable with Cinereous Vulture, but tail shape, black-striped underwing and pale head differentiate it. Adult has distinctive underwing pattern (half-white, half-black), but take care to rule out White Stork – distinguished by long neck and red bill, and long red legs protruding beyond tail. See Bearded Vulture for differences from that species.

▼ *Adult* ▼ *Subadult in flight*

▲ Adult ▲ Adult in flight

GRIFFON VULTURE *Gyps fulvus* 105cm, wingspan 230–265cm

Gregarious, colonial breeder on montane cliffs. Frequents most mountain ranges in Spain (except westernmost Cantabria and along the Mediterranean coast). Particularly common in Aragón and Castilla y León. Typically seen sailing high in the sky once the day has warmed up. Soars and glides on slightly raised wings with long, widely spaced 'fingers' at wing-tip; flaps with heavy, deep, slow wingbeats. Massive bird that dwarfs even large eagles. Upperwing distinctively two-toned (buff at front, dark at rear), contrasting with pale head and neck, and white stripes on underwing. These features distinguish it from rarer, all-dark Cinereous Vulture, which also glides with wings slightly inflected downwards.

CINEREOUS VULTURE *Aegypius monachus* 110cm, wingspan 250–285cm

Near Threatened; also called Black Vulture. Fairly common resident of wooded hills in the south-western quarter of Spain, notably Extremadura. Spain holds the vast majority of the European population. Huge bird, even larger than Griffon Vulture, which is the sole confusion species. More eagle-like shape than Griffon, as wings more evenly broad and head more protruding. Usually flies with slower, more deliberate wingbeats. Also has evenly black plumage, with only immature showing even a hint of Griffon's pale underwing. To rule out eagles, look for markedly short tail and more obvious 'fingers' to wing-tip, the outer two of which often curve upwards. Uniquely among vultures, comes into land with tail raised rather than with legs dangling.

▲ Adult in flight   ▲ Adult

SHORT-TOED SNAKE EAGLE *Circaetus gallicus* 66cm, wingspan 160–180cm

Fairly common summer migrant to most of Spain, wherever there is wooded terrain. Reptile specialist, favouring sunny, scrubby hillsides with short vegetation. Routinely hovers like a Common Kestrel, and soars on flat wings (slightly raised in other eagles and Common Buzzard). Very pale underparts differ greatly from those of most eagles, and most likely to prompt confusion with Common Buzzard, but much larger and longer-winged, and usually with a straight trailing edge to wing. Also lacks Common Buzzard's dark crescent on underwing (at carpal) and typically has well-spaced bars on undertail. At rest, looks noticeably large-headed with staring yellow eyes.

WESTERN MARSH HARRIER *Circus aeruginosus* 50cm, wingspan 120–135cm

Scattered breeding populations, particularly in the Ebro Valley, Castilla–La Mancha, Castilla y León and western Andalucía. More widespread and common in winter (particularly along coasts), when numbers swell with northern birds. Favours wetlands (particularly with reedbeds) but also hunts over agricultural land. Typically seen quartering low over vegetation, with steady, elastic wingbeats between glides on raised wings. Heavier and broader-winged than other harriers, but not as round-winged as buzzards. Straighter wings and rounded tail eliminate kites. Male attractive and distinctively tricoloured. Female and immature dark chocolate with variable cream patches on head, breast and wings. Striking spring display flight, including toe-to-toe food passes between male and female.

▼ Adult male   ▼ Adult female in flight

▲ Adult male in flight　　　　　　▲ Adult female in flight

HEN HARRIER *Circus cyaneus* 50cm, wingspan 100–120cm

Uncommon breeder in northern and west-central Spain. Fairly common throughout Spain in winter. Frequents wetlands, agricultural land and lightly forested areas. Typical harrier flight (see Western Marsh Harrier). Large raptor – but smaller and more slender than Western Marsh, and with quite different plumage (male ghostly, pale grey with black wing-tips; female/immature brown with a white rump and banded tail). Most similar to Montagu's Harrier (for differences, see that species). Female/immature also conceivably confusable with Common Buzzard, but latter has comparatively shorter, broader wings and very different plumage.

34

MONTAGU'S HARRIER *Circus pygargus* 45cm, wingspan 95–115cm

Common summer visitor to lowlands across much of Spain, particularly in the western half. Rare in the north and along coasts. Inhabits extensive cultivated plains. Slender, seemingly long-tailed harrier, confusable only with Hen Harrier (and vagrant Pallid Harrier, *Circus macrourus*; not illustrated and unlikely to be encountered). Slimmer wings than Hen, with more pointed wing-tip (showing four 'fingers' rather than Hen's five), and flight generally more buoyant. Male darker grey than Hen, with a longer black wedge on wing-tips and black stripe across upper- and underwings (latter plain white in Hen). Female very similar to female Hen in plumage; best distinguished by shape. Immature has unstreaked brick-coloured body and underwing (streaked and buff in Hen).

◀ From top: adult male, juvenile, adult male in flight

NORTHERN GOSHAWK *Accipiter gentilis* 50–64cm, wingspan 90–125cm

Shy, fairly common resident of large, undisturbed forests throughout most of Spain. Most likely to be seen in heavily wooded parts of the north; absent from non-forested land in the south. Most readily detected during late-winter display flight, when it flies slowly over woodland before plummeting. Significant gender size difference: male barely crow-sized, female almost the size of Common Buzzard. Differs from latter in long tail, bulging 'S' shape to rear wing and frequently pointed wing-tips (like those of Peregrine Falcon). Most similar to Eurasian Sparrowhawk and often misidentified as such. Most reliable differences are Northern Goshawk's larger size, deep chest, broad undertail (often fluffed out and gleaming white) and long head. Dark eye-mask, broad white stripe over eye and strongly barred underparts are visible in good views.

EURASIAN SPARROWHAWK *Accipiter nisus* 30–40cm, wingspan 60–80cm

Resident and common throughout most of Spain, wherever there is wooded habitat. Most common in the north; in the south, favours hilly areas and is absent from treeless terrain. Numbers are bolstered by northern birds in winter and by passage migrants. Hunts by surprise, flying fast and low, then streaking over fences and hedges to catch small birds unawares. Roughly the size of  Common Kestrel (females bigger than males), but has broad, rounded wings (rather than long, narrow and pointed). Flight intersperses rapid flapping with long glides; never hovers like Common Kestrel. Male blue-grey above with an orange-flushed face. Female (above) steel-grey above, finely barred white below. Immature brown with coarsely barred underparts (not streaked as in most falcons). Most similar to Northern Goshawk (for differences, see that species).

▲ First-winter in flight   ▲ Adult

COMMON BUZZARD *Buteo buteo* 52cm, wingspan 110–130cm

Very common raptor resident across the whole of Spain (although absent from the Balearics), frequenting any habitat with trees. Benchmark bird of prey when identifying other species. Large, with broad, rounded wings, often seen soaring buoyantly or sitting still on exposed perches such as posts. Shorter-tailed than Western Marsh Harrier and does not quarter low over ground like that species. Although plumage is variable (covering the spectrum from whitish to dark brown), consistent features include a broad, diffuse, dark trailing edge on underwing and, at best, a poorly defined tail-band. For differences from European Honey Buzzard, see that species. Often heard calling – a loud, sharp mewing that drops in tone.

SPANISH IMPERIAL EAGLE *Aquila adalberti* 78cm, wingspan 180–210cm

Vulnerable. Scarce resident – but much less rare than formerly, thanks to conservation action – of south-west quarter of Spain, including Madrid, Cáceres, Sierra Morena and Doñana. Favours dry, rocky pine woodland – particularly on hillsides – with a high density of European Rabbits (*Oryctolagus cuniculus*). Very similar to the more widespread Golden Eagle, but tail shorter (markedly less than width of wings). Soaring shape also differs: Spanish Imperial's wings are more evenly broad, with a straighter rear edge rather than bulging towards inner rear wing, and it glides on flatter wings. Prolonged views of an adult should also reveal the unique broad white leading edge to the inner forewing, which is particularly obvious when the bird is head on.

▼ Adult in flight   ▼ Adult

▲ Adult   ▲ Subadult in flight

GOLDEN EAGLE *Aquila chrysaetos* 85cm, wingspan 190–225cm

Resident of rocky areas in most mountain ranges, notably the Pyrenees and Ebro Valley. Circles sedately high in the sky, apparently with little effort. Much larger than the more familiar Common Buzzard, with longer, more bulging wings and head, and a squarer tail. Longer-tailed and longer-winged than other Spanish eagles. Largely dark plumage, although adult has a golden nape (making head appear pale at a distance), and immature has extensive white tail base and broad white flashes in wing.

BOOTED EAGLE *Aquila pennata* 47cm, wingspan 110–135cm

Common summer visitor and occasional winter visitor; resident in the Balearics. Frequents most of Spain, particularly in the south-west. Common in the Pyrenees and, particularly, the Strait of Gibraltar on migration. Inhabits extensive deciduous woodland, typically on slopes and with clearings. Small eagle – size of Common Buzzard – with short wings. Variable plumage, with light, dark and intermediate morphs. Dark morph recalls Black Kite (particularly given pale bar on upperwing) but differs in square tail, narrow white rump and less acrobatic flight. Pale phase (below) has contrasting underwing pattern like Egyptian Vulture – white at front, black to rear.

BONELLI'S EAGLE *Aquila fasciata* 60cm, wingspan 145–165cm

Resident; scarce and sparsely distributed. Most frequent along the Mediterranean coast and in Extremadura. Prefers warm, dry regions. Nests on cliffs, and often hunts over cultivated, open rocky areas such as *garrigue*. Larger than Common Buzzard and Booted Eagle; differs from both in being slender and long-tailed. Unlike those species, relatively consistent in plumage. Adult has a diagnostic white saddle; grey tail with broad, dark terminal band; and dark underwing contrasting with white belly. Largely pale plumage and smaller size distinguish it from Golden Eagle. Short-toed Snake Eagle differs in having bulging, broad wings; multiple bars on tail; and (typically) a dark chest bib.

LESSER KESTREL *Falco naumanni* 30cm, wingspan 63–72cm

Summer visitor to much of central and southern Spain, with some also wintering in the south. Particularly common in west Andalucía and Extremadura. Hunts over open areas but nests colonially on vertical, usually man-made structures. Smaller, slimmer and more elegant than Common Kestrel, perhaps with quicker, lighter wingbeats. Male Lesser differs from male Common in having a bluer head (lacking black moustache), unspotted chestnut back, blue-grey band across inner upperwing and almost white underwing. Female very similar to female Common, but possibly looking gentler thanks to paler cheek and lack of dark smudge behind eye. However, reliably distinguishable only on very close views, when pale (not black claws) of Lesser may be visible.

▼ *Adult male in flight*

▼ *Adult male*

▲ Adult male   ▲ Adult female

COMMON KESTREL *Falco tinnunculus* 34cm, wingspan 65–80cm

Spain's most common and widespread falcon, abundant in most open habitats, from urban areas to mountains. Largely resident, although numbers are boosted by winter arrivals. Falcons have long, slender wings and generally long tails. This is the benchmark falcon (see other species for differences). Frequently seen hovering before dropping to the ground like a stone to catch a small mammal. Also soars well, when it may prompt confusion with Eurasian Sparrowhawk, which has more rounded wings. Sitting upright on a post, looks front-heavy, tapering towards tail-tip. Male has a blue-grey head and brick-coloured mantle; female has a pale brown head with a heavily barred copper mantle.

EURASIAN HOBBY *Falco subbuteo* 32cm, wingspan 70–85cm

Uncommon summer visitor throughout northern and eastern Spain (with scattered enclaves elsewhere). Prefers open areas near wetlands and deciduous woodland, where it hunts aerial insects (particularly dragonflies) in aerodynamic flight. Slightly smaller than Common Kestrel but with markedly longer, more pointed wings and a long tail. Adult plumage very different to Common Kestrel, with prominent dark eye-mask contrasting with white neck, black-striped underparts, grey upperparts and rufous 'trousers'. Juvenile similar but with dark brown-grey upperparts and buff 'trousers'. Differs from Peregrine Falcon in smaller size, thinner wings, slimmer tail base, striped underparts and coloured 'trousers'.

▲ Adult ▼ Adult in flight

ELEONORA'S FALCON   *Falco eleonorae*   40cm, wingspan 90–105cm

Summer visitor, nesting in isolated colonies in the Balearics. Seen on the mainland, particularly the Mediterranean coast, on migration and before the breeding season (which it times to coincide with the southwards passage of landbirds in autumn). Agile hunter, targeting aerial insects and migrating birds. Typically glides on flat wings, with forceful wingbeats and searing bursts of speed. Roughly the size of Peregrine Falcon, but wings and tail longer, and body much slimmer. Closer to large Eurasian Hobby, but with even longer wings and tail, and dark underwing (whitish and barred finely in Eurasian Hobby). Plumage variable: has pale, intermediate and dark morphs.

PEREGRINE FALCON   *Falco peregrinus*   45cm, wingspan 90–115cm

Breeds widely across Spain, but unevenly distributed; most frequent in the east. Favours rocky or mountainous areas, including coasts. Largely a winter visitor in the south-west. Additional northern birds winter in Spain, often in grasslands and wetlands. Large, powerful falcon. Thick-necked, short-tailed and typically deep-chested, with broad-based wings narrowing rapidly to a fine tip. Accordingly, much stockier than any other Spanish falcon, and easily differentiated on shape. Plumage clean and striking, with blue-grey upperparts (browner in immature), finely barred white underparts and a clear-cut dark eye-mask on white face. Sits around for long periods before taking to the air in fast, direct chase with whippy wingbeats, often stooping to seize its victim.

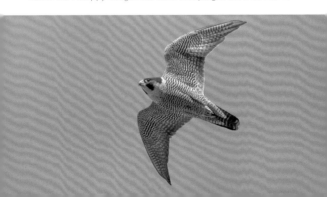

WATER RAIL *Rallus aquaticus* 25cm

Fairly common resident in lowland wetlands, marshes and other vegetated waterways throughout much of Spain. Population marginally boosted by wintering birds from further north. Rails, crakes and gallinules are small to medium-sized birds that creep shyly through dense waterside vegetation. Most are more often heard than seen. The Water Rail's piglet-like squeals can be rather alarming for the uninitiated. Slightly smaller than Common Moorhen, and distinctly pear-shaped, although larger than crakes (*Porzana* spp.; not illustrated). Most eye-catching feature is also diagnostic: a long, decurved red bill (short in all other members of the family).

COMMON MOORHEN *Gallinula chloropus* 29cm

Very common resident throughout Spain, except in mountains and arid regions. Population boosted by winter visitors from further north. Inhabits most types of waterbody, including canals and ponds in urban areas. Plump, with a small head and long legs. Bobs head when swimming, scuttling off if disturbed. Adult can be confused only with Eurasian Coot; unique features are red-and-yellow bill, large white patch under tail and white stripe along sides. Being brown, juvenile could be confused with juvenile Water Rail; differs in short brown (rather than long and red) bill, yellow (not red) legs, white side stripe and white undertail.

▼ *Adult*   ▼ *Immature*

PURPLE SWAMPHEN *Porphyrio porphyrio* 48cm

Resident, with populations scattered across central, southern and eastern Spain, plus Balearics. Frequents well-vegetated lakes. Shy species, rarely leaving the cover of reedbeds. When it reveals itself, size and coloration render it unmistakable. Much larger than Eurasian Coot – indeed, larger than ducks such as Eurasian Wigeon – and thickset, with a stocky neck and massive red bill and front shield. Plumage is iridescent purplish-blue with a contrasting white undertail. Distant birds – when size is hard to judge and plumage looks all dark – could conceivably be mistaken for Common Moorhen, but that species is much slighter, and has yellow (not red) legs and a white side stripe.

EURASIAN COOT *Fulica atra* 39cm

Common resident in wetlands throughout much of Spain, except in mountains. Winter numbers are boosted by arrivals from further north. Inhabits lakes and reservoirs; usually avoids smaller waterbodies (canals, ponds) frequented by Common Moorhen, the only confusion species. Substantially larger than that species, with wholly black plumage (lacking white on sides or undertail). Uniquely, bill and frontal shield are ivory white (rather than Common Moorhen's red and yellow). Staring red eye can lend an irate look – and members of a group of Eurasian Coots perpetually squabble with one another. Gawky on land, with legs set well back and fat, peapod-like toes. Runs across water to take off.

▲ Juvenile (left), adults (right)

▲ Adults in flight

COMMON CRANE *Grus grus* 95–120cm, wingspan 180–220cm

Locally common in winter (notably in Extremadura) and on passage, when it follows a trajectory between north-east and south-west, with a traditional stopover at Gallocanta. Such congregations provide one of Europe's most exciting avian spectacles. Tall, imposing, stately bird on the ground; appears immense and rectangular-winged in flight. Long-legged, slender-necked and small-headed. Size and mainly grey plumage may suggest Grey Heron, but taller and more slender, with adult's white blaze standing out on black head and neck. Wings also straighter and flapping more stiff – much more like a stork or vulture. Migrates by day. Very vocal – an evocative oboe-like *krrooo*.

LITTLE BUSTARD *Tetrax tetrax* 43cm, wingspan 83–90cm

Near Threatened. Resident in selected extensive cultivated plains; more widespread in winter. Still reasonably common (particularly in Extremadura), although populations are decreasing rapidly. Body size (i.e. without tail) roughly that of Common Pheasant (*Phasianus colchicus*; not illustrated, scattered populations released for hunting), and mottled brown females potentially confusable with that species, particularly if bird crouches semi-concealed in vegetation. However, lacks long tail of Common Pheasant, and has longer legs, a large head and a long, thick neck. During mating period, fully adult males display striking black-and-white neck ruff. In display, male throws back head and utters 'farting' call, occasionally jumping in air. Unmistakable in flight, with rapid duck-like beats of broad wings and blinding white outer wing etched black. For differences from Great Bustard, see that species.

▼ Adult male

▼ Adult female

▲ Adult male in flight　　　　　▲ Adult male

GREAT BUSTARD *Otis tarda* 75–105cm, wingspan 170–240cm

Vulnerable. Fairly common but declining resident of arid grassy and cultivated plains of central and southern Spain. Gregarious in winter. Huge – males are Europe's heaviest bird. Strongly built, with a stocky neck, deep chest, sturdy legs and long wings. Flies with deep, elastic and unhurried wingbeats, when its largely white wings avoid conceivable confusion with eagles or Common Crane. As majestic on the ground as it is in the air. Only likely to be mistaken for Little Bustard, but it dwarfs that species. Great's plain grey neck differs from that of female Little (mottled brown) and male Little (extensive black). In flight, both bustards have extensively white wings, but Great has largely pale wing-tips (dark in Little) and a broad dark border to rear wing (black dots in Little).

EURASIAN STONE-CURLEW *Burhinus oedicnemus* 42cm

Resident in much of Spain, but absent from the north and east, and from both mountainous and forested regions. An unusual wader that shuns water, typically inhabiting arid terrain with short or sparse vegetation. Camouflaged and reclusive, hard to spot and usually inactive by day. Size of Eurasian Oystercatcher, but has the slender shape of a long-winged, long-legged plover. At a distance, it looks white-faced, with a pale base to thick bill, features that soon differentiate it from European Golden Plover. In close views, look for long white band on folded wing and black tip to bill. In flight, uniquely patterned, markedly long wings appearing largely black against brown body, with striking white flashes.

BLACK-WINGED STILT *Himantopus himantopus* 35cm

Spain's most widespread breeding wader, being particularly common in the Ebro Delta and Guadalquivir. Mainly a summer visitor, with overwintering birds concentrating in the south-west. Habitat varies from freshwater wetlands to coastal saltpans. Unmistakable elegant, slender shorebird, with unfeasibly long strawberry-pink legs immediately betraying its identity. Wholly black upperwing and longish, needle-fine black bill additionally differentiate it from the only other black-and-white waders (Pied Avocet and Eurasian Oystercatcher). In flight, recalls a giant Green Sandpiper, but wholly white tail and long, bright legs avoid confusion. Juvenile/first-winter – with dull yellow-orange legs and brown upperparts – might be mixed up with other shorebirds (e.g. Common Greenshank); check leg length!

PIED AVOCET *Recurvirostra avosetta* 44cm

Sparsely distributed resident, with most of Spain's population in the south-west, particularly along the Guadalquivir Valley. Frequents shallow wetlands, muddy bays, lagoons and marshes. Large, easily recognised wader: no other species has such markedly piebald plumage and a long, thin, upturned bill. Eye-catchingly white in flight. Common Shelduck has a similar pattern, so potentially confusable at a distance and if size not apparent. Look for Pied Avocet's long, protruding bill and legs, wholly white rear wing (except black wing-tips), and lack of broad transverse band across breast and upper back. Has a unique feeding action, swishing bill from side to side. Black-winged Stilt has wholly black upperwings, and Eurasian Oystercatcher has wholly black head and neck, plus an orange bill and pink legs.

▼ *Adult*   ▼ *Adult in flight*

EURASIAN OYSTERCATCHER *Haematopus ostralegus* 42cm

Near Threatened. Rare breeder, with scattered populations in the
north-east and north. Scarce winter visitor along the Atlantic coast.
Equally at home on saltmarshes, sandy beaches, damp fields and
rocky shorelines. Highly vocal, often grabbing attention with loud,
strident piping. Large, stocky wader – one of the biggest. Black-and-
white plumage enables identification even at long range: wholly black
head distinguishes it from both Black-winged Stilt and Pied Avocet
(and has more extensive black upperparts than latter). Additionally
differs from these species in long, bright orange-red bill, and from
Pied Avocet in pink (not grey) legs. In flight, reveals a distinctive broad
white wing-stripe and white 'V' extending from uppertail to back.

COLLARED PRATINCOLE *Glareola pratincola* 25cm

Uncommon summer visitor, usually to open arid or saline areas, but
often near water. Largely occurs in south-west Spain, but also
scattered populations along the eastern coast. Usually seen either
standing alert or hawking for insects like a tern, but in the air, brown
wings and black tail rule out possible confusion with terns. On the
ground, somewhere between Little Ringed and European Golden
plovers in shape, but with an attenuated rear end due to long wings
and tail. Plumage distinctive, however, with buff throat-patch outlined
in black, and red base to short bill.

▼ *Adult in flight*   ▼ *Adult*

EUROPEAN GOLDEN PLOVER *Pluvialis apricaria* 27cm

Uncommon winter visitor and passage migrant on agricultural plains and short grassland. Particularly frequents south-west Spain; also common in the Balearics. Often in the company of Northern Lapwing. Medium-sized wader, much larger and more thickset than the ringed plovers but with a similar run–stop–pivot feeding action. In wavering flight, flocks shimmer gold and white, often calling (an evocative, mournful whistle). On the ground, spangled upperparts create an overall yellow-brown effect. In adults retaining or developing breeding plumage, face and most of underparts are variable black. Smaller and slighter than Grey Plover; for other differences, see that species.

GREY PLOVER *Pluvialis squatarola* 28cm

Coastal migrant and winter visitor (particularly to the Atlantic coast and Ebro Delta), favouring estuaries, rocky coasts and saltmarshes. Habitat thus usually different from that of the only confusion species, European Golden Plover, although latter can frequent estuaries and mudflats. Only marginally larger than European Golden, but appears noticeably stockier, heavier-billed and more lethargic. As name suggests, spangled upperparts give it a silvery impression, never yellowish as in European Golden. In flight, look for diagnostic black 'armpits' (wholly white underwing on European Golden). At a distance, could prompt thought of Red Knot (*Calidris canutus*; not illustrated, uncommon winter visitor to Atlantic coasts), but longer legs, shorter bill and run–stop–pivot foraging manner are all typical of plovers.

▲ Adult in flight

▲ Adult

NORTHERN LAPWING *Vanellus vanellus* **30cm**

Near Threatened. Scarce breeder on a few grassland areas, notably in Castilla–La Mancha and Castilla y León. Common and widespread in winter, frequenting plains and valleys throughout the country, but notably common in the south-west, along coasts and in the Balearics. As happy on dry land as in wetlands. Gregarious, stocky, distinctive plover. Bottle-green upperparts (can appear black at a distance or in poor light), largely black breast and pied head with a long, wispy crest (disproportionately so in breeding season). Typical plover feeding action (run–stop–pivot). Distinctive rolling flight on rounded wings, which are all dark above (contrasting with white band on tail) and emphatically bicoloured below. Calls include a distinctive wheezy *peee-wit*.

LITTLE RINGED PLOVER *Charadrius dubius* **17cm**

Fairly common summer visitor to freshwater bodies and gravel pits. Widespread – particularly inland – except in mountains. Rare winter visitor on the southern coast. Plovers have a distinctive feeding action, running rapidly and then standing stock-still. Small wader, the size of Common Starling, with the shape of an unripe pine cone (front-heavy, tapering to a fine tip). Plain-backed, with prominent markings on head and breast. Very similar to Common Ringed Plover; best told by plain upperwing in flight (Common has a long white stripe). Adult also differs in yellow eye-ring, dull straw legs (not orange) and black (not bicoloured) bill. Juveniles are trickier; Little has a darker head with indistinct (at best) stripe behind eye. See also Kentish Plover.

▼ Adult

▼ Juvenile

▲ *Adult male*　　　　　　　　　　▲ *First-winter*

COMMON RINGED PLOVER *Charadrius hiaticula* 18cm

Fairly common winter visitor to Atlantic and, to a lesser extent, Mediterranean coasts. Frequents shorelines, wetlands and estuaries. Rare inland. Very similar to Little Ringed Plover (for differences, see that species). Differs from Kentish Plover in bolder dark markings on head and breast (black in adult, brown in juvenile), particularly complete breast-band. Upperparts also markedly darker (Kentish appears pale). Adult has bright orange legs, and juvenile yellow (those of Kentish are dark, but can appear paler when muddy).

KENTISH PLOVER *Charadrius alexandrinus* 16cm

Fairly common resident along Mediterranean and Andalusian coasts, with enclaves on the north-west Atlantic coast and inland. Prefers sandy beaches and dunes, but also frequents mudflats. Inland, favours salt lakes. Slightly smaller than the two ringed plovers, but looks weedier (see Common Ringed Plover for differences). Less elongated than Little Ringed Plover. Adult male has more white and less black on head than adult male Little Ringed, and an attractive chestnut cap. Female and juvenile similar to juvenile Little Ringed; look for paler upperparts, paler patch on breast-sides, white wing-stripe in flight and lack of pale eye-ring.

▽ *Adult male*　　　　　　　　　　▽ *Adult female*

WHIMBREL *Numenius phaeopus* 41cm

Common migrant along Atlantic coasts, with occasional birds wintering. Prefers sandy or rocky coasts, plus saltmarshes and mudflats on migration. Large wader, marginally bigger and stockier than Black-tailed Godwit, but noticeably smaller than Eurasian Curlew. Like the latter, differs from all other large waders by strongly decurved bill. Compared to Eurasian Curlew, bill is shorter and more sharply decurved. Also, plumage is colder and darker, with prominent face pattern comprising dark eye-stripe and crown divided by pale band over eye and central crown-stripe. In comparison, Eurasian Curlew has a plain face on which black eye stands out.

EURASIAN CURLEW *Numenius arquata* 53cm

Near Threatened. Common winter visitor and passage migrant, particularly along Atlantic coasts. Very rare breeder in the north. Frequents mudflats, bays, estuaries and marshy grassland. By far Spain's largest wader, typically feeding singly or in loose groups. Very long, decurved bill distinguishes it from all waders except Whimbrel (for differences, see that species). In flight, like Whimbrel, could be confused with Bar-tailed Godwit (*Limosa lapponica*; not illustrated, common on passage along Atlantic coasts), showing similarly plain brown wings and a white 'V' on rump and lower back. However, Eurasian Curlew flight is typically more sedate than either species; focus on bill to rule out Bar-tailed Godwit.

▽ *Adult*

▽ *Adult*

▲ Adult summer   ▲ Adult winter

BLACK-TAILED GODWIT *Limosa limosa* 40cm

Near Threatened. Common in winter and on passage, particularly on Atlantic coasts and in major wetlands. Sporadic breeder. Equally at home on shallow estuaries, freshwater marshes and lagoons. Large wader, midway in size between Common Greenshank and Eurasian Curlew. Size, black legs and very long, almost straight bill eliminate almost all other waders. Spotted Redshank is easily excluded on leg colour (red). Eurasian Curlew and Whimbrel have strongly down-curved bills; Common Greenshank's is gently upcurved. In flight, striking white wing-bar recalls Eurasian Oystercatcher, but has a square white rump (not extensive 'V'). At rest, similar to Bar-tailed Godwit (*Limosa lapponica*; not illustrated, common on passage along Atlantic coasts) but larger and with straighter bill; in flight, striking wing pattern differs from Bar-tailed's solid brown wings.

RUDDY TURNSTONE *Arenaria interpres* 23cm

Winters on Atlantic coasts, particularly in the north-west and near Cádiz, but more widespread on passage. Favours rocky shores and pebbly or sandy beaches with ample seaweed. Busy but inconspicuous wader, rummaging over seaweed-strewn tidelines, flipping stones and detritus in search of concealed invertebrates. Stocky and short-legged, with a short neck and small head. Focus on the underside to identify this species: no other shorebird possesses the combination of orange legs, white undertail and belly, black breast, and short, sharply pointed, triangular bill. Dingy grey-brown in winter plumage (below) but summer adult is smart, with largely chestnut upperparts and a white-and-black head. Stripy in flight, with wing-bars and three white lines along back.

SANDERLING *Calidris alba* 20cm

Common winter visitor and migrant along the Atlantic coast, rarely on the Mediterranean coast. Frequents tidelines of sandy and shingle beaches, or rocky shores; rarely on mudflats. Distinctive foraging behaviour, sprinting beside waves parallel to tideline and pecking at food while on the go (rather than standing and probing, like Dunlin). Similar in size to Dunlin, but bill shorter. Winter-plumaged adult is glaringly white on head and underparts, with pale grey upperparts. Juvenile has spangled upperparts like a young Dunlin; best differentiated by wholly unmarked underparts (Dunlin has streaking on breast). In flight, has a mostly grey rump and tail (Dunlin's rump is white with a dark central line).

DUNLIN *Calidris alpina* 19cm

Very common wintering and migrant wader, particularly along Atlantic coasts. Scattered pockets on the Mediterranean coast (notably the Ebro Delta) and sometimes inland. Often in flocks of thousands. Frequents estuaries, rocky coasts and marshes. Low numbers inland. Starling-sized, grey-brown and common, Dunlin is the benchmark for identifying small waders. Smaller than Red Knot (*Calidris canutus*; not illustrated, uncommon winter visitor to Atlantic coasts) but larger than Little Stint, and with a longer bill than both. Smaller than Curlew Sandpiper (*C. ferruginea*; not illustrated, uncommon in autumn on Mediterranean coasts), with a

shorter, straighter bill and a black line down rump (rather than a wholly white rump). Summer adult and juvenile have more heavily marked underparts than similar waders: black belly in former, streaked breast in latter. See Sanderling and Little Stint for differences from those species. Regularly calls in flight: a scratchy *preeee*.

▲ Adult summer　　　　▲ Juvenile

LITTLE STINT *Calidris minuta* 15cm

Common passage migrant and uncommon winter visitor, mostly to coasts and to south and east Spain. Appears dainty, moves rapidly. Most likely to be confused with Dunlin, compared to which it is even smaller (sparrow-sized), with a shorter, straight (rather than downcurved) bill. Size differentiates it from the larger Sanderling, as do its habits, as latter usually seen sprinting along tidelines. As a rule of thumb, bill is about as long as head; Dunlin's is much longer. Temminck's Stint (*Calidris temmincki*; not illustrated, scarce migrant) is as tiny as Little, but has pale legs (not black) and plainer upperparts, and moves by shuffling unobtrusively.

RUFF *Calidris pugnax* 22–32cm

Common passage migrant (particularly in spring) across the country, both inland and on the coast. Scarce winter visitor, mainly in Doñana. Frequents wet grasslands, marshes and muddy lagoons; prefers freshwaters. Very variable wader that causes much confusion. Male half as large again as female; sometimes bigger than Common Redshank but always slimmer, shorter-billed and more elegant. Larger and slimmer than Red Knot (*Calidris canutus*; not illustrated, uncommon winter visitor to Atlantic coasts), with a longer neck and legs. Uniquely among Spanish waders, juvenile typically has unmarked apricot-buff underparts. Female typically brown with yellow-orange legs. Non-breeding male plumage varies from whitish to dusky brown; in nuptial finery, any colour goes! Flight rather stiff on long wings, revealing, uniquely, white ovals on rump.

▽ Adult male　　　　▽ Juvenile

EURASIAN WOODCOCK *Scolopax rusticola* 36cm

Uncommon breeder in old-growth forests of the north. Widespread and common in winter, when it favours woodland or nearby damp fields and ditches. Fundamentally nocturnal, typically seen when flushed by day or flying over at dusk. In breeding areas, gives a distinctive, flickering display flight (roding) at treetop level, alternately croaking and uttering a sharp, teeth-sucking *tsiwick*. Cryptic brown-and-buff plumage blends in with leaf litter; very hard to spot on the woodland floor. Much larger and more pot-bellied than Common Snipe, with a comparatively shorter, thicker bill. Face also less stripy, with black bands across crown, and has consistently barred (rather than partly striped) underparts and lacks Common Snipe's pale tramlines on back.

COMMON SNIPE *Gallinago gallinago* 26cm

Rare, localised breeder. More widespread and very common on migration and in winter – particularly on coasts. Favours well-vegetated wetlands, hiding in dense cover or feeding inconspicuously nearby with sewing machine-like probing. Size of Common Redshank but fatter, with short legs and immensely long bill. Heavily striped head and back are distinctive. Camouflaged plumage comprises stripes, bars and crescents. Flies off urgently when nervous, typically uttering a harsh *kartch*, and powers off into distance, zigzagging and towering. Much larger than rarer Jack Snipe (*Lymnocryptes minimus*; not illustrated, widespread, particularly on coasts) and rarely bobs like that species. See Eurasian Woodcock for differences from that species.

COMMON SANDPIPER *Actitis hypoleucos* 20cm

Uncommon resident, breeding on inland rivers, gravel pits and shallow freshwater lakes – particularly in hilly areas in the north. Seen more widely on migration (when common) and in winter, including on coasts. Wader the size of Dunlin, with nondescript brown-and-white plumage. Behaviour, however, is distinctive. Moves with a nervous, straining gait, bobbing elongated rear end constantly like a wagtail (*Motacilla* spp.). Feeds with darting motions and regular changes of direction. Upperparts paler brown than Green Sandpiper and plainer than spangled Wood Sandpiper. Differs from both in white 'hook' on breast-sides. No chance of confusion in flight; often flickering, with white wing-bar, and dark rump and tail centre. Distinctive loud, ringing calls, particularly in flight: *swee-wee-wee*.

GREEN SANDPIPER *Tringa ochropus* 22cm

Winter visitor to freshwater wetlands; widespread. More common on migration. Starling-sized wader, slightly larger than similar Common Sandpiper. Tubbier and less elongated than Common, with slower movements and only occasional bobbing. Looks dark and white (more contrasting than Common), particularly in flight as both upper-and underwings are wholly dark and square rump is white (Common has noticeably white wing-stripe and dark rump). Also, has a finely speckled back (rather than plain). If disturbed, often flies high and distant, uttering a high-pitched *klu-wi-wi*; can recall a giant Common House Martin! See Wood Sandpiper for differences from that species.

SPOTTED REDSHANK *Tringa erythropus* 31cm

Fairly common migrant throughout Spain, particularly along coasts.
Also winters in small numbers in major wetlands. Generally feeds
alone, wading through deepish water. Long red legs discount all
waders except Common Redshank. Larger than the latter, and in
winter/juvenile plumage (above) is grey rather than brown (in
summer garb, uniquely jet black). Prominent white line over eye
differentiates it from Common (which has a relatively plain face). In
flight, appears all dark with an isolated white oval on rump; lacks
Common's white triangle at back of wing. If leg colour is unseen in
flight, confusable with Common Greenshank, but has a dark tail (not
largely white) and an emphatic disyllabic call: *chui-uit*.

COMMON GREENSHANK *Tringa nebularia* 32cm

Thinly distributed on migration, mostly along coasts but also inland.
More clearly coastal in winter, when rarer. Frequents freshwater
lagoons, marshes and estuaries, typically wading leggily through
water too deep for most shorebirds. Tall, long, elegant wader with
greyish plumage. Bigger and greyer than the distinctly brown
Common Redshank, with pale yellow-green (not bright red) legs and
uniformly dark wings (lacking broad white triangle). Leg colour
differentiates it from similar-sized Spotted Redshank. Also lacks the
latter's white line above eye and bill is slightly upcurved rather than
straight (with no red). Call is a loud, ringing, unhurried *diu-diu-diu*.

WOOD SANDPIPER *Tringa glareola* 20cm

Common spring and autumn migrant along the east coast and in the Balearics. Rare elsewhere. Frequents freshwater wetlands, including flooded fields and muddy ponds. Smaller than Common Redshank, with yellow (not red) legs. Size of Common Sandpiper but legs and neck longer, so it looks more elegant and happier wading through water. Differs from both Common and Green sandpipers by spangled back, and long white band extending well behind eye. In flight, all-dark upperwing and white rump distinguish it from Common, but upperwing is clearly paler than in Green (mid-brown, not blackish) and underwings are greyish (not blackish), so it looks much less contrasting. Flight call is a trisyllabic *kif-kif-kif*.

COMMON REDSHANK *Tringa totanus* 26cm

Local breeder in major wetlands, mostly inland. Common winter and passage visitor to coasts, favouring estuaries, marshes, damp grasslands and bays. An alert, active, boisterous wader: often bobs head and flees noisily at slightest hint of danger (uttering a loud, nervy *diu-u-u*). Bright red legs mean confusion is possible only with Spotted Redshank (for differences, see that species), although yellow-legged birds might occasionally be mistaken for Common Greenshank (see that species). A good species to become familiar with, as it facilitates size comparisons with other waders, thereby aiding identification.

▲ Adult in flight

▲ Adult

LITTLE TERN *Sternula albifrons* 23cm

Summer visitor, breeding along Mediterranean and Andalusian coasts, but also inland, particularly in Extremadura. Seen on migration along all coasts. Favours beaches, islands and saltpans. Terns are smaller and slimmer than gulls, with a thin, pointed bill and sharply angled wings. Little Tern is a tiny tern that flies rapidly on long, angular wings. Feeds belligerently, with rapid hovering followed by a vertical plummet, smashing through the water surface. Size and shape distinguish it from other terns, but, at close range, also look for two unique features: discrete white forehead and extensively yellow bill.

GULL-BILLED TERN *Gelochelidon nilotica* 40cm

Uncommon summer visitor, breeding on fringes of wetlands and hawking insects over open areas. Patchily distributed, both inland and on the coast. Closely resembles similarly sized Sandwich Tern, but shorter wings, thicker neck and shorter bill produce a different jizz in flight. Seen at close range, bill is all black, lacking yellow tip of adult Sandwich. At rest, visibly longer-legged than Sandwich. Feeding behaviour also differs: never plunges into water (like Sandwich), but hawks, dips or swoops over water or dry land. In winter plumage, Gull-billed has a broad, dark eye-mask (like Mediterranean Gull), which differs from narrow black stripe extending back from eye to ear crown in Sandwich. Call also differs: a low, harsh *ker-wik*.

▽ Adult in flight

▽ Adult

WHISKERED TERN *Chlidonias hybrida* 26cm

Fairly common but localised summer visitor, breeding in scattered wetlands, mainly in southern and eastern Spain. Favours shallow waterbodies with floating vegetation, and is the marsh tern most likely to be seen in Spain. Whiskered Terns fly into the wind, often in small groups, dipping down to the water surface to grab food; like other marsh terns they never dive. Summer adult (above) unmistakable: mainly ash grey, with contrasting white cheeks and a neat black cap, this smart attire neatly set off by a blood-red bill. Dark underparts (in summer adult) and pale grey, barely forked tail (in all plumages) rule out Common Tern.

SANDWICH TERN *Sterna sandvicensis* 40cm

A recent coloniser in Spain and now a scarce breeder in the Ebro Delta and València. Widespread and common along all coasts during migration; rare in winter. Frequents shingle beaches, offshore waters, coastal lagoons and mudflats. A fairly large, pale grey tern with long wings and a short tail. Shape is the quickest way to differentiate it from other terns such as Common Tern, which is slighter, slimmer-winged and longer-tailed. At close range, adult Sandwich reveals a unique yellow tip to black bill and a shaggy black crest (rather than a neat cap). Very vocal: a loud, grating *ki-urr-ik*. Fishes at sea, diving from on high with a resounding splash.

▲ *Adult winter* ▼ *Juvenile in flight*

▲ Adult in flight

▲ Adult

COMMON TERN *Sterna hirundo* 35cm

Fairly common summer visitor, breeding in wetlands, gravel pits and lagoons, particularly along the Mediterranean coast. More common and widespread on migration; rare in winter. Medium-sized tern, much larger than Little Tern (for differences, see that species) but smaller than Sandwich Tern. Adult distinctive, with a long, forked tail; neat black cap; and red bill. Juvenile has pale basal half to bill, unlike all-black bill of Sandwich. Differs only very subtly from the mainly coastal Arctic Tern (*Sterna paradisaea*; not illustrated), which is almost exclusively seen on migration.

BLACK-LEGGED KITTIWAKE *Rissa tridactyla* 40cm, wingspan 93–105cm

▲ Adult in flight
▼ First-winter in flight

Vulnerable. Exclusively coastal, with a couple of breeding enclaves in Galicia. More widespread along all coasts on passage and in winter, but often stays offshore, unseen, unless blown in by storms. Delicate pelagic gull, with airy flight even in strong wind. Adult can be confused only with Common Gull (*Larus canus*; not illustrated, scarce winter visitor to coasts) of same age. Looks much neater than that species, with prominent, wholly black wing-tips (as if dipped in ink) and an unblemished yellow bill. In winter, can show dusky smudges on head – but never streaked as in Common Gull. First-winter is distinctive, with a broad black collar on hindneck, black zigzag across wing, and black tip to tail that gives it the illusion of being forked.

▲ Adult

▲ Adult in flight

SLENDER-BILLED GULL *Larus genei* 40cm, wingspan 90–102cm

Scarce, localised resident of coastal wetlands (particularly saltpans) in Cataluña, València and Andalucía. Delightful, elegant gull, often seen delicately picking insects off the water surface. Only confusion species is the abundant Black-headed Gull; although Slender-billed is larger, it is also noticeably longer and more slender, with a distinctive profile comprising a thinner neck, elongated head and long bill. Adult is wholly white-headed (Black-headed always has at least a dark spot behind eye). First-winter very similar to first-winter Black-headed; dark marks on plumage are fainter, but best identified by different shape. Audouin's Gull is larger than Slender-billed with (in adult) a thick, largely red bill.

BLACK-HEADED GULL *Larus ridibundus* 37cm, wingspan 86–99cm

Breeding colonies scattered throughout Spain, particularly on the Mediterranean coast but also in occasional inland wetlands. Very common and widespread in winter, mainly on the coast but also inland (including in urban areas such as Madrid). The default small gull; getting to know this bird helps identify more exciting species. Adults have a unique chocolate-brown head in summer, but a less distinctive dark ear spot in winter. In flight, look for long white triangle on upperwing 'hand' and neat black trailing edge: only Slender-billed Gull has a similar pattern (for differences, see that species). Adult Little Gull (*Hydrocoloeus minutus*; not illustrated, migrant along coasts) is smaller, with a smoky underwing and black bill. First-winter Black-headed resembles adult winter but has variable dark wing markings and a black tail-tip. See Mediterranean Gull for differences from that species.

▽ Adult summer in flight

▽ Adult winter in flight

▲ Adult summer in flight   ▲ Adult winter

MEDITERRANEAN GULL   *Larus melanocephalus*   39cm, wingspan 94–102cm

Mainly seen in winter and on passage, particularly on the Mediterranean coast; rare inland. Breeds only occasionally. Favours freshwater bodies, saltmarshes, bays and sandy shores. One of the smaller gulls, between Black-headed and Common gulls (*Larus canus*; not illustrated, scarce winter visitor to coasts) in size. More robust than the former, particularly in flight. Adult is distinctive – the only gull with unblemished, wholly pale grey/white wings and a red bill (Black-headed has black on wing-tip and underwing). White (not smoky) underwings, larger size and bill colour distinguish it from adult Little Gull (*Hydrocoloeus minutus*; not illustrated, migrant along coasts). In winter, at all ages, prominent, dark eye-mask differentiates Mediterranean Gull from Common and Black-headed. Summer adult has a unique jet-black hood with white eye crescents.

AUDOUIN'S GULL   *Larus audouinii*   48cm, wingspan 117–128cm

Increasingly common resident along the Mediterranean coast, including the Balearics. Breeds on islands, in salt-pans and in harbours. A conservation success story, having once been among the world's rarest gulls. In shape, recalls a small, attenuated and slender-winged European Herring Gull. Protracted sloping forehead culminates in a thick bill. All plumages have grey legs, which rules out most gull species. Adult is attractive, with clean white, grey and black plumage topped off by a blood-red bill with a black subterminal band and yellow tip (like summer adult Mediterranean Gull). Younger plumages rather scruffy and best identified on shape (long, droop-tipped bill and long wings) and leg colour.

◀ From top: adult in flight, second-winter, adult

LESSER BLACK-BACKED GULL *Larus fuscus* 52–58cm, wingspan 117–134cm

Very common in winter, along coasts and inland (e.g. Madrid, Extremadura). Has recently started breeding at sites along the eastern coast. Usually slightly smaller than European Herring Gull. Most adults have a coal-grey back and wings – darker than in adult European Herring or Yellow-legged gulls, but paler than in adult Great Black-backed Gull (*Larus marinus*; not illustrated, scarce winter visitor to coasts). Adult also differs from the latter by much smaller size and yellow legs. Leg colour also distinguishes it from European Herring (but, self-evidently, not Yellow-legged!). First-winter has a more coarsely marked back and wing, blacker bill and, typically, whiter head than European Herring of same age.

EUROPEAN HERRING GULL *Larus argentatus* 54–60cm, wingspan 123–148cm

Scarce winter visitor to northern Atlantic coast, and occasionally elsewhere. Large gull, although smaller than Great Black-backed Gull (*Larus marinus*; not illustrated, scarce winter visitor to coasts). Among large gulls, adult has the palest back and wings. Pink legs additionally differentiate it from Yellow-legged and Lesser Black-backed gulls. Second-winter confusable with Common Gull (*Larus canus*; not illustrated, scarce winter visitor to coasts), but much larger. First-winter variable, but generally less coarsely marked than Lesser Black-backed of same age and less white-headed than that species or Yellow-legged. Former also has a contrasting, wholly black wing-tip.

▷ *From top: first-winter in flight, third-winter, adult*

▲ Adult   ▲ Second-winter

YELLOW-LEGGED GULL *Larus michahellis* 52–58cm, wingspan 120–140cm

Very common resident along coasts, particularly in the north. Increasingly being seen inland. Adult differs from European Herring Gull in lead-grey back/wings (not pale grey) and yellow legs (not pink). Adult Lesser Black-backed Gull shares yellow legs but has darker back/wings. First-winter is most similar to Great Black-backed Gull (*Larus marinus*; not illustrated, scarce winter visitor to coasts) of same age, sharing white head and stocky all-black bill, but has a bolder black tail-band. First-winter has darker wings and whiter head than first-winter European Herring, and is larger and cleaner-headed than first-winter Lesser Black-backed.

BLACK-BELLIED SANDGROUSE *Pterocles orientalis* 36cm

Uncommon and rapidly declining resident of lowland arid plains over a wide area of Spain, particularly in the Ebro Valley, southern plains and Extremadura. Sandgrouse are stocky, fast-flying pigeon-like birds of open grassland. They are wary, and are usually seen flying in groups over grassland, often calling, before disappearing when they land. Both of Spain's species are largely brown above, with long, sharply pointed wings that are contrastingly black and white underneath – features that eliminate confusion with pigeons or doves. Black-bellied Sandgrouse is named after its key identification feature: a solid black belly and vent (these areas are white on Pin-tailed Sandgrouse), easily seen in flight. Black-bellied is also easily discerned (indeed, picked up) by its bubbling call.

▼ Adult male   ▼ Adult female

PIN-TAILED SANDGROUSE *Pterocles alchata* 30cm

Resident populations are scattered across Spain, but uncommon and decreasing. Most frequent in Aragón and La Mancha. Habitat as for Black-bellied Sandgrouse. Similar in appearance to Black-bellied but with a clean white belly and vent, so appears much paler underneath in flight. Both sexes have protruding tail feathers ('pin-tail') and this feature – along with harsh, grating call – further differentiates them from Black-bellied. At close range, this is a beautiful bird, with an orange face and chestnut breast-band.

ROCK DOVE/FERAL PIGEON *Columba livia* 32cm

Feral Pigeons are abundant through lowland Spain, particularly in urban areas. Birds resembling pure ancestral Rock Doves (from which Feral Pigeons descend) breed on cliffs in the Balearics, and along southern and eastern coasts. Rock Doves are smart birds, compact and neatly plumaged, with a triangular white rump contrasting with grey wings (featuring two black wing-bars) and a black-tipped grey tail. Feral Pigeons, in contrast, are avian ragamuffins – thick-necked and stocky, often hobbling on deformed feet. They vary dramatically in plumage, with any combination of white, grey or black complemented by purple or green sheens.

▲ Adult in flight   ▲ Adult

STOCK DOVE *Columba oenas* 30cm

Fairly common resident in the north-eastern half of the country, with birds wintering further south and west. The smallest true pigeon, neatly proportioned and smartly attired. Flies with rapid, deep beats of wings that lack the broad white band that characterises Common Wood Pigeon. Iris is black rather than white (Common Wood Pigeon) or orange (Feral Pigeon), creating a beady-eyed impression. Also distinguished by shiny green neck collar (white on adult Common Wood Pigeon) and short black double wing-bar. Voice distinctive: long, disyllabic cooing, repeated once a second.

COMMON WOOD PIGEON *Columba palumbus* 40cm

Very common resident throughout Spain except in high mountains. Abundant in winter, particularly on agricultural plains, and on migration through Pyrenean passes. Breeds in any wooded habitat, from lowland forests to urban gardens (where it is increasingly prominent). The largest pigeon, fat chested, broad-winged and with a waddling gait. Clatters into flight, clapping wings noisily. Size alone is sufficient to eliminate other pigeons, but diagnostic plumage feature is obvious in flight: broad white bar cutting across wing. Adult also has a white iris and extensive white patch on collar – characteristics shown by no other pigeon or dove.

EURASIAN COLLARED DOVE *Streptopelia decaocto* 31cm

Unknown in Spain before 1960; has since colonised rapidly to become very common, particularly along coasts. Favours gardens, parks and farmland. Large dove, the size of Rock Dove/Feral Pigeon, but slimmer and longer-tailed. Plumage is distinctive at rest: unmarked, wholly buff-grey with black-and-white neck collar (absent in juvenile). More likely to be confused with European Turtle Dove in flight, with similarly contrasting wings and white tip to tail. However, latter feature is much broader than on European Turtle. Familiar song: a trisyllabic, mournful *ou-ou-whoo*.

EUROPEAN TURTLE DOVE *Streptopelia turtur* 27cm

Vulnerable. Fairly common resident throughout parts of lowland Spain, although declining rapidly and now scarce in many areas. Breeds in open deciduous woodland, copses, and farmland with ample hedgerows. The smallest dove or pigeon, and the most colourful and boldly patterned. Plumage unique, with a boldly chequered orange back and wings, largely pink head and underparts, and a neck collar comprising several black-and-white lines. In flight, looks colourful above and has a narrower white band on tail-tip than Eurasian Collared Dove. Song is a prolonged, subdued purring.

MONK PARAKEET *Myiopsitta monachus* 30cm

Originally from South America, this species escaped from collections and is now widely distributed across Spain. Locally common, it favours cities (Barcelona, Madrid, Málaga, Palma de Mallorca, València, etc.) and eastern Spain. Its predominantly green coloration distinguishes it from all native Spanish species except European Green Woodpecker. However, that species has a different shape, with a long bill and head, but short tail; it also has a bounding flight, unlike the parakeet, which flies rapidly and directly. Beware confusion with Rose-ringed Parakeet (*Psittacula krameri*; not illustrated, uncommon in major urban areas). Monk has a shorter tail, extensive grey on both head and breast, and a whitish (not pink) bill, and lacks Rose-ringed's pink collar.

GREAT SPOTTED CUCKOO *Clamator glandarius* 37cm

Fairly common summer visitor across most of Spain bar the north and extreme south; most frequent in the centre and south. Inhabits Mediterranean lowlands with scattered trees. Recognisably cuckoo-like, but big, gawkish and rather clumsy. Very long wings and graduated tail give it a flight shape like no other Spanish species. Plumage also distinctive. Adult unmarked whitish below (unlike Common Cuckoo, which has a grey face and breast and barred belly), with blackish upperparts stippled and barred white (plain grey in Common Cuckoo). Juvenile (below) similar but browner, with a neat black cap and eye-catchingly rufous outer wing.

▲ Adult

▲ Adult in flight

COMMON CUCKOO *Cuculus canorus* 34cm

Common summer visitor throughout Spain, although avoids arid, treeless and urbanised areas. Frequents a wide variety of open-country and wooded habitats – wherever the birds it parasitises reside. Easier to hear than see. Indeed, best known for male's song: two-toned, with the second note lower, *cu-cou*. In flight, recalls both pigeons and falcons, but long tail is often spread, and broad-based wings taper rapidly to a fine point. Often perches prominently, with long wings dropped and tail cocked. Male plumage ash-grey with a barred belly; female similar but has a barred breast, perhaps recalling Eurasian Sparrowhawk (although latter perches upright, and has a white eyebrow and stockier body).

BARN OWL *Tyto alba* 33–39cm, wingspan 80–95cm

Common and widespread throughout lowland Spain, particularly in plains, valleys, marshes, farmland and villages in southern and central regions. Often breeds in old or rarely used farm buildings. Familiar, easy-to-identify owl – appears glowing white when quartering low over fields in the darkening evening. White face, underparts and underwing remove confusion with any other owl. Warm beige upperparts, suffused grey, are also unique. Eerie vocal repertoire comprises hisses, shrieks and squeals.

▽ Adult

▽ Adult in flight

EURASIAN SCOPS OWL *Otus scops* 20cm, wingspan 47–54cm

Common summer visitor throughout Spain, particularly near coasts. Scarce in the north and in mountains. Very small owl, the size of a Common Starling. Even smaller than Little Owl (sole confusion species), but has a different shape and posture – slender, standing upright – and long ear-tufts. Latter, plus dark 'V' on forehead (plummeting to bill) and fine lines on underparts, also differentiate it from Little. Voice characteristic of balmy southern nights: liquid *piou*, whistled every couple of seconds.

EURASIAN EAGLE-OWL *Bubo bubo* 60–75cm, wingspan 138–170cm

Fairly common resident throughout most of Spain, but absent from Cantabria, the north-west and intensively cultivated regions. Favours undisturbed natural areas, far from human habitation, particularly rocky cliffs. Strictly nocturnal, emerging at dusk, when male and female call to each other: a deep *bou-hou*. Massive owl, larger than Common Buzzard. Size alone distinguishes it from other family members: thickset, big-headed and broad-winged. If seen perched in torchlight (or roosting bird encountered by day), orange eyes and ear-tufts differentiate it from all bar the much-smaller Long-eared Owl.

LITTLE OWL *Athene noctua* 23–27cm, wingspan 50–57cm

Common and widespread
resident, particularly in hot (even
arid) regions. Favours farmland,
grassland, meadows and wooded
parkland. Frequently seen sitting
on walls and ruined buildings.
Often active by day as well as
night. Small, round owl: in Spain,
only larger than Eurasian Scops
Owl (for differences, see that
species). Broadly striped underparts, white eyebrows and white-
blotched upperparts are distinctive. In bounding flight, wings
and tail appear noticeably short.
Sometimes stands erect with legs
outstretched, even running after
prey. Song is a rhythmic *keeeah*.

TAWNY OWL *Strix aluco* 37–43cm, wingspan 81–96cm

Common resident throughout most of Spain, inhabiting forests, parks
and wooded countryside. Densities vary; most common in the north
and in wooded regions, and rarest in arid, treeless terrain. Nocturnal;
only rarely encountered by day (but look out for angry tits and finches
mobbing one). Best known for its voice – a quavering hoot, *hou-ouuu*
(*twit tu-woo*), and a sharp *kee-wik*! When perched, shape is very
different from elongated Barn Owl or Long-eared Owl, being dome-
headed, thick-bodied and short-tailed. In flight, has a large head and
broad-based wings. Plumage includes mottled browns, buff and
white, but can look disconcertingly pale in car headlights.

LONG-EARED OWL *Asio otus* 34cm, wingspan 86–98cm

An uncommon resident that occurs pretty much throughout Spain, inhabiting forests, hedgerows near grasslands, and parks. It is most common in central and southern regions. Roosts in dense cover by day, hunting at night. At rest, is a tall, upright owl with long ear-tufts – quite unlike Tawny Owl. Eyes, if open, are a vivid orange, like those of much larger Eurasian Eagle-owl. In flight, appears longer-winged than Tawny, with barred buff 'hand' on upperwing and isolated black comma at 'elbow' on underwing. Differs from rarer Short-eared Owl in barred (not solid black) wing-tips and orange (not yellow) eyes. Juvenile makes a call like a squeaky gate; adult's song is a rhythmic, muffled *hou* every couple of seconds.

SHORT-EARED OWL *Asio flammeus* 37cm, wingspan 95–105cm

Scarce winter visitor across much of Spain bar the far north. Also a rare breeder in north-central regions, locally common in years with large vole populations. Favours damp grasslands, where (unlike typical Long-eared Owl) it hunts by day – although most frequently seen at either end of the day. Similar to the more frequent Long-eared Owl, but larger, with solid black wing-tips, short ear-tufts and plain (rather than streaked) belly. At close range, yellow eyes can be discerned (orange in Long-eared). In flight, appears longer and slimmer-winged than Tawny Owl, and with clearly buff-based (not brown) plumage. Smaller and buffier than Eurasian Eagle-owl.

▼ *Adult in flight*   ▼ *Adult*

EUROPEAN NIGHTJAR *Caprimulgus europaeus* 26cm

Uncommon summer visitor to the northern half of Spain in particular. Rarely overlaps with Red-necked Nightjar. Inhabits sandy heaths with scattered trees, particularly pines. Strictly nocturnal – although may be spotted roosting or be flushed by day. Emerges at dusk, male singing with a vibrating churr that lasts minutes. Size of European Turtle Dove, but slim-bodied and with long wings and tail. Shape apparent when at rest – sitting horizontally on ground, branch or log – and in silhouetted flight (when it recalls a small falcon); in contrast, all owls are round-bodied with a vertical posture. Seen by torchlight, male has conspicuous white spots on wing-tip and tail corners; in daylight, plumage is revealed to be mottled brown and buff. For differences from Red-necked Nightjar, see that species.

RED-NECKED NIGHTJAR *Caprimulgus ruficollis* 32cm

Common summer visitor to open, particularly sandy woodlands in dry lowlands. Favours the southern half of Spain, so comparatively little overlap in range with the sole confusion species, European Nightjar. Like that species, also has white spots near wing-tip and at tail corners, but bigger and noticeably longer-tailed (size and shape are best way to distinguish the two in the dark). By torchlight or in daylight, look for Red-necked's rusty collar, and four rows of white dots on folded wing (rather than European's single line). Most easily differentiated by voice: in contrast to European's long, vibrating churr, female Red-necked gives a hoarse, chugging call like a steam train and male's song is a hollow, disyllabic knocking.

COMMON SWIFT *Apus apus* 18cm

Abundant summer visitor throughout Spain, particularly in the north. Distribution constrained only by suitable habitat for breeding (cliffs, buildings, etc.) – although feeds far from nest over all manner of open areas. Swifts resemble swallows and martins, but are larger, with long, pointed, scythe-like wings. They fly rapidly (as their name suggests), searing high through the sky, often in noisy, screaming groups. As well as shape, all-dark underparts remove confusion with Barn Swallow etc. – and Common Swift never perches on wires. High-flying bird could possibly be confused with similarly shaped Eurasian Hobby, but much smaller and has wholly dark underparts. To distinguish it from other swifts, see those species.

PALLID SWIFT *Apus pallidus* 17cm

Common summer visitor to eastern and southern coasts, with breeding pockets inland. Rare in the north but may be overlooked. Behaviour and habitat like those of Common Swift, which is most likely confusion species. The two are *very* hard to tell apart. Subtle plumage differences include black eye and dark eye-mask standing out against a paler head in Pallid, larger and more diffuse white throat, paler brown upperwing (such that darker saddle can stand out) and scaly underparts (visible at close range). In shape, Pallid has a slightly blunter wing-tip and broader hand – but even experts struggle to differentiate between the two species.

ALPINE SWIFT *Apus melba* 22cm
. . . .
Uncommon summer visitor, breeding colonially on cliffs (whether in mountains or by the sea) or cliff-like structures. Fragmented distribution, mostly in the east but scattered throughout Spain; rare in the north. Resembles Common Swift in shape and flight, but markedly larger, longer-winged and more powerful. Plumage is also very different, with mid-brown upperparts similar in tone to Sand Martin and much paler than other swifts. Underparts also recall Sand Martin, with white throat-patch (sometimes hard to see) and white belly isolated by broad brown collar and undertail. Call also differs from other swifts' screaming: a mechanical, chattering *ti-ti-ti-ti-ti*.

COMMON KINGFISHER *Alcedo atthis* 18cm
. . . .
Fairly common resident throughout Spain except in mountains and the arid south-east. Numbers somewhat boosted by arrival of northern birds in winter. Frequents rivers, streams and lakes, as long as there are banks in which it can excavate a nesting tunnel. Unmistakable, even in typically brief view – a blurred flash of electric blue as the bird speeds low over water, attracting attention with a strident *tsiiiiii*. Smaller than Common Starling, and noticeably stocky, with a long dagger of a bill. Scintillating blue upperparts and warm-orange underparts, with a white throat and half-collar on neck.

▲ Adult male   ▲ Adult in flight

EUROPEAN BEE-EATER *Merops apiaster* 27cm

Summer visitor throughout most of Spain, particularly abundant in the south and absent only from the north. Favours open areas with abundant insects and exposed perches from which to hunt; needs sandy banks for nesting burrows. Unmistakable harlequin of a bird, roughly the size of European Turtle Dove, with long, pointed wings and a central spike to rounded tail. At close range, appears multicoloured, although impression at a distance may be of chestnut upperparts, electric-blue underparts and pale underwing. Often in flocks, which attract attention with noisy, rolling *prrrp* calls. Acrobatic feeder, tumbling and twisting after insects.

EUROPEAN ROLLER *Coracias garrulus* 30cm

Uncommon, declining summer visitor, mainly to southern Spain, particularly Extremadura and the arid south-east. Favours open, dry environments with scattered trees. Attractive bird that is slightly smaller than Western Jackdaw, but more thickset and with a heavier head and bill. Confusion possible only with silhouetted birds; when bright coloration is seen, it is unmistakable. Neon-blue head, underparts and forewings are unique in Europe, and gloriously offset by a rich chestnut back. Usually perches prominently well above ground, on telegraph wires for example, looking for beetle and grasshopper prey. Distinctive slow, powerful flight on broad, sharply angled (and largely blue) wings. Juveniles are duller and faintly streaked, but nevertheless distinctive.

HOOPOE *Upupa epops* 27cm

Summer visitor throughout Spain except the far north (where it is absent). Very common resident in the south (north to Extremadura) and along the Mediterranean coast. Frequents open country with hedgerows and scattered trees. Another unmistakable bird, whether waddling along the ground mechanically probing with its long, decurved bill, or flopping in butterfly-like flight on eye-searingly stripy wings. In flight, black-and-white bands and bars catch the eye. On the ground, can be surprisingly discreet, stripes blending into grass (rather like a zebra!) and pinkish upper body merging into stony ground. Crest is usually kept flattened, but occasionally erected, corona-like. Song is a fluty, repetitive *poo-poo-poo* – audible from a considerable distance.

EURASIAN WRYNECK *Jynx torquilla* 17cm

Fairly common summer visitor to northern half of Spain (although absent in the extreme north and north-west). Resident in the Balearics, in parts of the south and along the Mediterranean coast. Frequents orchards, scrubby hedgerows, and clearings in woodland. Often sits motionless for long periods in a bush or tree, relying on its camouflage to deceive predators. Feeds by hopping on the ground, almost thrush-like. Ostensibly a woodpecker, but you wouldn't know it, given its odd behaviour and almost owl- or nightjar-like plumage. In a good view it is unmistakable: look for dark eye-stripe, and dark stripe in centre of pale grey back. Song is a nasal, Common Kestrel-like *ki-ki-ki-ki-ki*, with up to 20 notes in five seconds.

EUROPEAN GREEN WOODPECKER *Picus viridis* 33cm

Very common, widespread resident. Particularly numerous in northern and central Spain. Absent from much of Extremadura and Andalucía. Frequents open environments with occasional trees, lightly wooded terrain and parks. Often seen on the ground, hunting for ants, or in deeply swooping flight. Spain's sole green woodpecker, and confusable only with non-native parakeets that occur in some cities (e.g. Monk Parakeet). Green plumage rules out smaller thrushes, which also feed on the ground. The subspecies that occurs in Spain (*sharpei*) is often considered a distinct species, called Iberian Green Woodpecker. It has a greyer head than birds of the nominate race, lacks their black eye-mask and calls differently.

GREAT SPOTTED WOODPECKER *Dendrocopos major* 25cm

Common across much of Spain, particularly in the north, but scarce or absent from arid regions and the eastern coastal strip. Inhabits forests, woodlands, parks and gardens. Eye-catchingly piebald woodpecker the size of a Common Blackbird. Often attracts attention with abrupt

tchik or drumming (in spring). Covers long distances in bounding flight, when white shoulder-patch is most visible. Similarly black-and-white Common Magpie is much larger with a very long tail. See Middle Spotted Woodpecker for differences from that species. In some areas, rarer woodpeckers (not illustrated) are worth considering: Lesser Spotted Woodpecker (*Dendrocopos minor*; widespread but uncommon away from coasts) is much smaller, with an extensively barred white back and white (not red) undertail; White-backed Woodpecker (*D. leucotos*; local in the Pyrenees) has a white rump rather than a white shoulder-patch.

MIDDLE SPOTTED WOODPECKER *Dendrocopos medius* 21cm

Scarce resident of isolated areas in extreme northern Spain (particularly Cantabria, Castilla y León, Palencia and Álava), where it favours old oak trees in warm locations. Somewhat smaller than Great Spotted Woodpecker, the main confusion species. Both birds are black, white and red, notably sharing broad white shoulder-patches. Middle Spotted differs in shape, being more squat, with a rounded head and short bill. Differs also in red (rather than black) crown and whiter face (notably, black stripe falls well short of bill). The underparts are extensively streaked (plain on Great Spotted) and the vent is washed pink (rather than stridently scarlet). Unlike Great Spotted, does not drum; instead, it defends territory with a whining, nasal song, a little like a slowed-down Common Kestrel call.

DUPONT'S LARK *Chersophilus duponti* 18cm

Near Threatened. A scarce, declining resident with a localised distribution, principally in north-central Spain. A sought-after species for many birdwatchers! Runs between low, sparse thickets (gorse, thyme, etc.) on dry, flat, stony or sandy ground. Best located during songflight, typically performed at dawn and dusk: melancholy opening notes are followed by whistles and a nasal miaow. On the ground, shy and hard to see. When it is glimpsed, however, identity is usually obvious as it is the only Spanish lark with a long, downcurved bill. Shape also distinctive: short-legged, short-tailed and long-necked. In flight, lacks Eurasian Skylark's pale trailing edge to upperwing. Moreover, pale underwing rules out both Crested Lark (underwing rusty) and Calandra Lark (underwing black).

CALANDRA LARK *Melanocorypha calandra* 19cm

Common resident of extensive agricultural plains in Spain's interior. Absent from much of the Mediterranean coast and the north. A large, hefty lark – noticeably stockier than Eurasian Skylark. On the ground, very thick bill and bold black patches at side of breast catch the eye. Both are diagnostic, with only Greater Short-toed Lark coming close on the latter feature. Can be confusing when seen in flight from below, with unique black undersides and white trailing edge to broad wings prompting thought of an adult Little Gull (*Hydrocoloeus minutus*; not illustrated, migrant along coasts). Song rather like that of Eurasian Skylark, but display flight's slow wingbeats give the impression of a bird simply hanging in the wind.

GREATER SHORT-TOED LARK *Calandrella brachydactyla* 15cm

Common but rapidly declining summer visitor, throughout much of Spain south of the northern uplands. Particularly abounds along the Mediterranean coast. Breeds in dry, open areas with bare ground, including cultivation. A small, pale lark that may prompt thought of a female House Sparrow as much as a Eurasian Skylark. Streaked crown and upperparts rule out House Sparrow. When crouching, typically looks sandy and whitish, with dark bands on wings. Differs from all other Spanish larks except the much bigger Calandra Lark in its almost entirely unmarked white underparts. Shows only a hint of black on breast-sides (unlike bold pattern of Calandra). Lack of long crest rules out Crested Lark, Thekla Lark and Eurasian Skylark.

LESSER SHORT-TOED LARK *Calandrella rufescens* 14cm

Common resident, but declining. Gregarious inhabitant of arid, bare ground in eastern Spain, principally in the Ebro Valley and extreme south-east. Spain's smallest lark, rather recalling a dwarf Eurasian Skylark, but with a stubbier bill and bolder face pattern, and lacking a crest. Most similar to Greater Short-toed Lark, but streakier than that species, both on the back and – critically – the breast. If you get a close look, check the wing-tip: if you can see the black primaries extending beyond the buffy tertials, it's a Lesser Short-toed (on Greater Short-toed, the longer tertials cloak the primary tips). Call is a buzzy trill, rather like that of Sand Martin.

CRESTED LARK *Galerida cristata* 17cm

Occurs throughout most of lowland Spain, except the northern strip and Balearics. Favours open, stony environments, from roadsides and railway lines to waste ground and vineyards. Slightly smaller than Eurasian Skylark, and appears slimmer and sandier in coloration. A closer look reveals a long crest that ends in a point and is often raised vertically (short and usually flattened in Eurasian Skylark), a noticeable white stripe above eye, and a long, slightly decurved bill (stubby and straight in Eurasian Skylark). In flight, looks shorter-tailed than Eurasian Skylark, with a rusty underwing and no white trailing edge to wing. Very similar to Thekla Lark; see that species for differences. Call is a fluty, melodious *tu-tee-tou*.

THEKLA LARK *Galerida theklae* 17cm

Very common resident, particularly in the south-east, in dry mountains and in the Balearics. Gets gradually rarer as you go north or west. Favours dry, bushy terrain, often on slopes; avoids the non-natural habitats often frequented by Crested Lark. Differs from Eurasian Skylark in long, pointed crest, thicker bill and bolder black streaking on breast against a clean white background. Very similar to Crested Lark; close views are often needed to distinguish the two. Look for Thekla's greyish (rather than rusty) underwing in flight, chestnut (rather than sandy-brown) tone to rump, thicker bill, and more distinct breast streaking. Unlike Crested Lark, Thekla regularly perches in bushes and trees.

WOODLARK *Lullula arborea* 15cm

Common resident, widespread in Spain in dry, open, lightly wooded environments. Absent from the Cantabrian coast, the arid south-east and treeless regions. Smaller than Eurasian Skylark, neater and more rounded, and with a shorter tail. The latter is particularly apparent in flight, when rounded wings are also obvious. Plumage similar to Eurasian Skylark, but look for bolder patterning on back, broad white stripe over eye, ginger ear-coverts, and diagnostic white–black–white pattern on leading edge of wing. Creeps inconspicuously over ground, flying away at the last moment. Song is repetitive, melodic and liquid; a beautiful sound. Call is a distinctive, yodelling *tle-wee*.

▲ Adult male   ▲ Adult female

EURASIAN SKYLARK *Alauda arvensis* 17cm

Widespread resident of agricultural fields, meadows and other open areas. Common in the north, but scarce in warmer regions of the south, the Mediterranean coast and the Ebro floodplain. Gregarious in winter, when numbers swell with arrivals from northern countries. Larger and bulkier than a sparrow, with broad wings obvious in stuttery flight. Closest in appearance to Crested and Thekla larks and Woodlark (for differences, see those species). Take care also to rule out Corn Bunting, which has a long tail and very deep bill; and Meadow Pipit, which is smaller, slighter, longer-tailed and thinner-billed. In flight, white trailing edge to wing is diagnostic. Gives a guttural, chirruping call; song is famous for its length and melodious trilling.

SAND MARTIN *Riparia riparia* 12cm

Fairly common summer visitor to lowland Spain. Distribution fragmented; favours major rivers and is particularly abundant in floodplains of the Duero and Ebro. More widespread and common on migration, especially around fresh-water bodies. Swallows and martins (hirundines) are aerial insectivores, feeding acrobatically with the aid of long, pointed wings and forked tails. Sand Martin is the smallest hirundine in Spain, smaller than a sparrow although looking larger in flight due to long wings. Brown plumage is shared only by Eurasian Crag Martin. Differs in having striking white underparts partitioned by broad brown breast-band (concolourous drab grey-brown in Eurasian Crag). The band is apparent at a distance, so also eliminates other hirundines. Pattern recalls Alpine Swift, but that species is much larger and longer-winged.

▲ Adult ▼ Adult in flight

▲ Adult in flight

▲ Adult

EURASIAN CRAG MARTIN *Ptyonoprogne rupestris* 14cm

Widely distributed summer visitor, particularly to upland areas. Scarce in winter, when it occurs particularly in the south and along coasts. Inhabits craggy areas with cliffs for nesting. Being brown, this hirundine can be confused only with the smaller, slighter Sand Martin (for differences, see that species). In flight, from below, 'armpits' are contrastingly dark. From above, white tail spots are diagnostic – particularly obvious when tail is spread. Rather stiff-winged in flight compared to other hirundines, appearing less dexterous.

BARN SWALLOW *Hirundo rustica* 17–19cm

▲ Adult ▼ Adult in flight

Very common summer visitor throughout Spain, including mountainous regions. Particularly abundant on migration. Rare in winter in the south. Frequents open areas, but also seen in towns and routinely hunts insects over freshwater bodies. The most familiar hirundine, with a slinky flight and long streamers on forked tail. Pale underparts rule out Common Swift, which is also larger and has much longer, narrower wings. Dark throat and wholly dark upperparts (no white rump) rule out Common House Martin. Red-rumped Swallow is more similar; see that species for differences.

▲ Adult   ▲ Adult in flight

COMMON HOUSE MARTIN *Delichon urbicum* 14cm

Very common summer visitor throughout Spain, including in mountains (where it breeds on cliffs) and urban areas (where it nests on buildings, hence the name). Also often seen hawking insects over freshwater bodies. Rare in winter in the south. Small hirundine, between Sand Martin and Barn Swallow in size. See both species for differences, but, fundamentally, broad white rump separates it from all Spanish hirundines except Red-rumped Swallow. Differs from latter in short, broad, forked tail (not long and spike-like), dark ear-coverts (head is blue-black and white, not chestnut and blue) and lack of any rufous on upper rump.

RED-RUMPED SWALLOW *Cecropis daurica* 16–17cm

Summer visitor to southern Spain, with the odd enclave elsewhere. Generally scarce, but very common in the south-west. Typically frequents open hillsides, nesting on cliffs or buildings. Barn Swallow-like shape, with long tail-streamers, rules out martins. (For additional differences from Common House Martin, see that species.) Most confusable with Barn Swallow. In flight, glides more stiffly than that species, with less manoeuvrability. Tail shape also differs, with less wispy long feathers often suggesting a single spike. This impression is exacerbated by dark (not white) undertail, so that tail looks stuck on. In plumage, pale rump (white and rufous) and isolated dark cap are quite different to those of Barn.

▲ Adult in flight ▼ Adult male

TAWNY PIPIT *Anthus campestris* 17cm

Fairly common summer visitor to north-central Spain in particular, but also the mountainous south. Favours short grassland and bare ground. Pipits are small, streaky, largely ground-dwelling birds that walk and scurry around. Pipits are smaller and slimmer than larks, and with thinner bills. Very similar in appearance to one another, pipits demand careful examination. Tawny Pipit is one of the most distinctive Spanish pipits, being large, slender, long-tailed, pale and relatively unstreaked. Its sandy upperparts are almost unstreaked, and it often scampers around with a wagtail-like horizontal posture. Its most prominent plumage feature – a broad white stripe above eye – also distinguishes it from Spain's other pipits.

TREE PIPIT *Anthus trivialis* 15cm

Fairly common summer visitor to the northern third of Spain, up to foothills (and sometimes higher). Passage migrant elsewhere, including in the Balearics. Frequents forest edges, wooded clearings and tree-strewn meadows. Tree Pipit is generally yellower than Meadow Pipit, particularly on breast, which contrasts with white belly. Stripe above eye is more pronounced, and often shows a pale spot at rear of ear-coverts. Unlike Meadow, sings from a tree – or at least starts/ends songflight from a tree. Call is a buzzy, breathy *skeeeez* – very different from Meadow's weedy *sip*.

MEADOW PIPIT *Anthus pratensis* 14.5cm

Near Threatened. Abundant winter visitor throughout Spain; also abounds on migration. Occupies any open, grassy country, whether damp or dry. Variable pipit, with birds toned greyish, brownish or olive depending on age and time of year. Some look clean-cut and neat, others dingy and streaky. Gregarious in winter, feeding in active, nervous flocks that spit into the air, flying weakly. For differences from Tree Pipit and Water Pipit, see those species. Take care not to mistake it for Eurasian Skylark (for differences, see that species) or Corn Bunting (which is larger, tubbier and deep-billed).

WATER PIPIT *Anthus spinoletta* 17cm

Breeds commonly in montane meadows of northern Spain. Widespread in winter, at low density, frequenting lowland marshes, grasslands and rivers. Larger than Meadow Pipit and Tree Pipit. Distinctive summer plumage, with a blue-grey head marked by a bright white stripe over eye (supercilium), unstreaked grey-brown back and pink flush to largely unmarked underparts. In winter plumage, more similar to Meadow and Tree, but differs in having black (not pink) legs, a more boldly patterned head (with a prominent white supercilium), and diffusely streaked, markedly white underparts with neither a hint of yellow nor black stripes.

▽ *Adult summer*   ▽ *Adult winter*

▲ *Adult male* ▲ *Adult female*

GREY WAGTAIL *Motacilla cinerea* 18cm

Uncommon resident in northern Spain and upland areas of the south. In winter, more widespread, visiting urban areas. Always associated with water: streams and rivers year-round, but also lakes and the like in winter. Wagtails are long-tailed pipit-like birds that run and canter along the ground, wagging their tail up and down. Grey Wagtail is distinctive: no other wagtail has an isolated, bright yellow wrap-around rump, vent and undertail that contrasts with white belly. Ash-grey back (rather than olive) additionally distinguishes it from Yellow Wagtail – and habitat differences are also useful. Largely grey face, lacking black on crown, separates it from White Wagtail.

YELLOW WAGTAIL *Motacilla flava* 17cm

Fairly common summer visitor to central Spain and along most coasts. Inhabits meadows, grasslands, marshes and farmland (but never riverbanks like Grey Wagtail); absent from arid areas. Breeding birds are of the subspecies *iberiae*, known as Spanish or Iberian Wagtail. Male recalls female Grey Wagtail, but has a bluer head, blacker ear-coverts, green back and wholly yellow underparts; among other features, lacks male Grey Wagtail's black throat and both sexes' contrasting yellow rump. Female is a faded version of male, with green upperparts, faded yellow underparts and a bold white stripe above eye differentiating it from female Grey. On passage, other subspecies may be seen, notably Blue-headed (*flava*), the male of which differs by having a pastel blue head and yellow throat.

Yellow (*flavissima*) may also be seen; male's green-and-yellow head is distinctive. Immature differs from White Wagtail of same age in dark face and lack of breast-band.

◀ *Adult male* flava
▼ *From left: adult male* flavissima, *adult male* iberiae

▲ Juvenile

▲ Adult male

WHITE WAGTAIL *Motacilla alba* 18cm

Resident throughout Spain; numerous in the north but scarce towards the south (where it is largely restricted to mountains). More widespread and abundant in winter. Breeds in rural environments (often near farms), but winters in fields near watercourses, often in urban areas. Differs from other wagtails in being wholly monochrome in all plumages. Adult distinctive, with white face flanked by black crown and black bib. Immature could be confused with Yellow Wagtail of same age, but has a pale face (and thus prominent eye) and (often blotchy) black bib (particularly contrasting in male). Most birds have a pale grey mantle (White Wagtail, subspecies *alba*), but black- or dark-grey-backed birds of the British race (Pied Wagtail, *yarrellii*) also occur rarely on passage or in winter in northern and western Spain.

WHITE-THROATED DIPPER *Cinclus cinclus* 18cm

Fairly common resident in northernmost Spain and a few other hilly areas; otherwise very localised. Inhabits fast-flowing rivers; indeed, never seen away from flowing water. Stocky, short-tailed bird, shaped like a Winter Wren but twice the size. Bobs on rocks, flies with whirring wings (often uttering a rasping *dzit* call), swims buoyantly, and (uniquely among Spanish songbirds) dives or walks underwater. Adult unmistakable: look for extensive white bib sandwiched between chestnut head and very dark belly. Juvenile – grey and mottled – may cause confusion, but combination of shape and habitat is distinctive, and adults are usually also present.

WINTER WREN *Troglodytes troglodytes* 9.5cm

Very common resident throughout Spain, from sea-level to upper altitudinal limit of forest in mountains. Abundant in the north, but rather mountain-dependent in the south. More widespread in winter. Inhabits any kind of undergrowth: bushes and hedgerows in open areas, shrub layer in gardens and woodland. Tiny bird, with a distinctive short, cocked tail and loud voice. Typically skulking, and more often heard than seen. Gives a variety of scolding, rasping and rattling calls. Song is amazingly loud and vibrant, combining warbles and trills. Differs from Dunnock and (scaly brown) juvenile European Robin in smaller size; short, cocked tail; and broad cream stripe above eye.

DUNNOCK *Prunella modularis* 14cm

Fairly common resident in northern Spain, but otherwise breeds only in isolated mountains in central Spain and the Sierra Nevada. More widespread and common in winter, favouring dense undergrowth. Size of European Robin, but longer-tailed and gait is usually horizontal. Relatively nondescript, frequently unobtrusive bird that can confuse the unwary. Behaviour distinctive: creeps through vegetation or shuffles over open ground, flicking tail. Much more heavily streaked than pipits (*Anthus* spp.), with extensively grey face and throat. Bold streaking rules out warblers such as Eurasian Blackcap. See Winter Wren for differences from that species. Similar in plumage to House Sparrow, but has a fine black bill (thick and often pale in House Sparrow) and boldly patterned (not plain) underparts.

ALPINE ACCENTOR *Prunella collaris* 18cm
. . . .

Scarce overall, but locally common breeder in mountainous regions (above 1,800m) in the north, particularly the Pyrenees and Picos de Europa, where it favours scree and alpine meadows. Occurs at slightly lower elevations in winter, when it is more widespread. Larger, tubbier relative of Dunnock, with similar plumage. Unlike Dunnock, prefers open terrain and is typically fearless. Size and behaviour are initial clues that this is not a Dunnock. Next, look for yellow base to bill, pronounced white spots on wing, black-and-white speckled throat, and broad streaks on belly and flanks (rufous in adult, ruddy brown in juvenile). Poor views might suggest another high-altitude specialist, White-winged Snowfinch, but that species has extensive white on wings.

RUFOUS-TAILED SCRUB ROBIN *Cercotrichas galactotes* 16cm
. . . .

Uncommon, rapidly declining summer visitor to scattered areas of southern Spain. Frequents orchards, vineyards and olive groves in dry Mediterranean lowlands. Favours dense shrubbery, often near buildings, but usually seen bounding around on the ground, jerking its tail vertically or spreading it open. A distinctive bird, rather like a long-tailed, long-legged Common Nightingale. Most noticeable feature is the tail, which is long, splayed and strikingly chestnut, with black-and-white spots at its tip. Even in a brief flight view, this is sufficient to identify the bird. Striking face pattern is usually obvious: a broad white stripe above eye, with narrow black lines through and below eye.

EUROPEAN ROBIN *Erithacus rubecula* 14cm

Common breeder in northern Spain; restricted to mountains further south. In winter, abundant and widespread thanks to arrivals from further north in Europe. Favours woodland, copses, hedgerows, scrub, parks and gardens. Robins and chats are small insectivorous birds with slim bills, and are usually seen on or near the ground. European Robin is a very common, familiar bird. Adult's extensive orange face and bib eliminate confusion with all other species. Juvenile may cause confusion, lacking orange and being scaly on head, back and underparts. However, the presence of a parent should confirm identification.

COMMON NIGHTINGALE *Luscinia megarhynchos* 16cm

Summer visitor throughout Spain except the far north. Most frequent in non-arid parts of the Mediterranean fringe. Frequents woodland and scrub with dense undergrowth. Well known for its remarkable song – long, melodious and fluid – often given at night. Secretive and skulking, but sometimes feeds in the open on the ground (typically cocking its long tail) and often sings from a prominent perch. Larger and longer-tailed than European Robin, and lacks orange bib. Upperparts warm brown, more rufous on tail, with creamy-brown underparts. Most likely to be confused with female Common Redstart (which has whiter underparts and an obvious red tail) or Garden Warbler (different shape, and grey-brown plumage with no hint of a rufous tail).

▲ *Adult male summer*   ▲ *Adult female*

BLUETHROAT *Luscinia svecica* 14cm

Uncommon breeder (subspecies *azuricollis*, the male of which has a wholly blue throat) in various scrubby uplands of the north-western quadrant of the country. More northerly subspecies (*cyanecula* and *namnetum*) winter locally in southern Spain and along the Mediterranean coast, favouring scrubby reedbeds, ditches and meadows. Resembles European Robin in size, shape and behaviour, although often skulking. Male is unique, with a bright blue bib. All plumages differ from almost all other birds in having a broad white stripe over eye and chestnut sides to tail (flashed in low flight). Confusion possible only between Sedge Warbler (*Acrocephalus schoenobaenus*; not illustrated, frequent on passage across Spain) and female/first-winter Bluethroat, but former has a different shape, all-brown tail and entirely plain underparts (female/first-winter Bluethroat always has a dark collar on breast).

BLACK REDSTART *Phoenicurus ochruros* 14cm

Resident in most of Spain, but winter visitor to some areas, notably the south-west. Very common and widespread in winter. Typically favours rocky areas (an exclusively montane breeder in the south), but also towns and villages, where buildings substitute for cliffs. Slightly larger and slimmer than European Robin, with a long reddish tail that it quivers constantly. Favours open areas more than Common Redstart and behaves more like a wheatear (*Oenanthe* spp.), routinely feeding on the ground. Male is unmistakable, with sooty-grey plumage and a white wing-flash. Female resembles Common, but dingier grey-brown and with less rufous on rump.

▼ *Adult male*   ▼ *Adult female*

▲ *Adult male*   ▲ *Adult female*

COMMON REDSTART *Phoenicurus phoenicurus* 14cm

Scarce summer visitor with a fragmented distribution, mostly in northern Spain. More common and widespread on migration. Favours open woodland, parks and forest edges. Tends to be arboreal – often elusive in the canopy. Adult summer male differs from Black Redstart in having four-colour plumage, with a black throat, white face, ash-grey back and orange underparts. To distinguish female from female Black Redstart and Common Nightingale, see those species. Young and winter-plumaged males resemble adult female, but have an orange breast and flanks, and a dusky throat. Reddish tail avoids confusion with all other species.

WHINCHAT *Saxicola rubetra* 13cm

Scarce, decreasing and local summer visitor to northern third of Spain; widespread and common on migration. Favours grassland and other meadows with bushes on which to perch. Size of European Robin but with a short tail. Typically perches on a bush – always upright and alert, and often flies at first hint of danger. Attractive bird. Male is particularly striking: boldly patterned upperparts, bold white stripe above eye on otherwise blackish face, and orange breast. Confusion likely only with European Stonechat (for differences, see that species). Face pattern might prompt confusion with Northern Wheatear, but latter is larger, with a grey back and largely white rump and tail.

▽ *Adult male*   ▽ *Adult female*

▲ Adult male   ▲ Adult female

EUROPEAN STONECHAT   *Saxicola rubicola*   12.5cm

Common resident throughout most of Spain, except in arid or
cultivated terrain. Common in winter, particularly along coasts and in
the south-west, when numbers are swollen by arrivals from the north.
Frequents natural open environments such as heathlands and
scrubby grassland; often associated with gorse. Likely to be confused
only with Whinchat, which is similar in size and behaviour. However,
differs in all plumages by lacking Whinchat's white stripe over eye and
white sides to tail. Male European Stonechat has a large white neck-
patch below black head, enabling identification at long range.

NORTHERN WHEATEAR   *Oenanthe oenanthe*   15cm

Fairly common summer visitor, particularly to uplands. Widespread in
the north, but restricted to mountains in the south. Migrants can be
seen anywhere. Frequents open habitats, particularly dunes, short
grassland and stony meadows. Wheatears are terrestrial species,
venturing only marginally above ground to perch on a rock or fence.
Northern Wheatear has a distinctive feeding action, sprinting a short
distance before standing erect. Often flies when observer approaches,
flashing large white rump and tail (latter with an inverted black 'T'). This
rules out all species except Black-eared Wheatear. Male differs from
latter in blue-grey back (not white or peach), while female has less
white on tail than Black-eared, is paler above and lacks orange breast.

▽ Adult male   ▽ Adult female

 Adult male   ▲ Adult female

BLACK-EARED WHEATEAR *Oenanthe hispanica* 14cm

Fairly common summer visitor, but declining. Restricted to open ground in dry, hot regions, particularly in the south and east. Smaller and slighter than Northern Wheatear. Routinely terrestrial but more readily perches on bushes than Northern. Male distinctive, with apricot crown and back rather than Northern's blue-grey, and more extensive black wings (due to contiguous black scapulars). Some males also differ in displaying a black throat (only ear-coverts are black in Northern). Females and immatures are harder to differentiate. Focus on tail pattern: Black-eared's tail has black sides (white in Northern) but is otherwise more extensively white.

BLACK WHEATEAR *Oenanthe leucura* 17cm

Scarce and localised resident, largely in the south and east – particularly the arid south-east. Tied to dry, rocky areas, and often found around abandoned buildings, atop which it readily perches. A hefty, pot-bellied wheatear, larger than Northern Wheatear. Often pumps tail up and then down. Unmistakable plumage. Male is coal black (female sooty brown) all over except for white vent, rump and most of tail. Other all-black songbirds such as male Common Blackbird and Common Starling are differentiated on shape and in lacking extensive splash of white.

COMMON ROCK THRUSH
Monticola saxatilis 19cm
. . . .

Scarce summer visitor to scree-rich mountains in the northern half of Spain (where locally common) and upland Andalucía. Rock thrushes recall both wheatears (*Oenanthe* spp.) and thrushes (*Turdus* spp.), and are exclusively associated with warm, rocky places. Male Common Rock Thrush is a gorgeous creature, whose bright colours ensure it cannot be mistaken for anything else. Female is more subtle; most have an orange wash to scaly underparts that excludes both the larger Song Thrush and female Blue Rock Thrush. Both of these species are also excluded by the short, red-sided tail that protrudes only marginally beyond wing-tip.

▷ *From top: adult male summer, adult female, adult male winter*

BLUE ROCK THRUSH *Monticola solitarius* 20cm
. . . .

Uncommon resident of rocky places in Spain, although its distribution is fragmented. More frequent in the east and south, being rare and localised in the north. More widespread (and at a lower altitude) in winter. To distinguish it from Common Rock Thrush, see that species. Although wholly dark, shimmering blue in colour, the male Blue Rock Thrush can look black at a distance – at which point it might be confused with a male Common Blackbird. Female Blue Rock also recalls a female Common Blackbird (although lacks reddish tones and is markedly scaly). In both instances, Blue Rock's long black (not yellow) bill, dark (not pink) legs and smaller size are key to identification.

▽ *Adult male*   ▽ *Adult female*

▲ Adult male   ▲ Adult female

RING OUZEL   *Turdus torquatus*   25cm

Scarce resident of mountainous regions in the north (Pyrenees, Cantabria), with passage migrants in the east and a decent wintering population in the south-east. Breeds in open conifer forests, but migrants use a variety of open grassy habitats. Medium-sized, mainly dark thrush, confusable only with Common Blackbird and Mistle Thrush. Adults differ from both these species in broad bib (white in male, buff in female), silvery wings (particularly obvious in flight) and scaly underparts. Also much darker than Mistle Thrush, with a yellow (rather than largely dark) bill.

COMMON BLACKBIRD   *Turdus merula*   24cm

Abundant resident throughout Spain, with the population supplemented by arrivals from the north in winter. Inhabits a variety of habitats containing trees and bushes. Familiar medium-sized thrush, running or hopping along the ground and then stopping to look for prey. All-black male confusable only with crows and choughs, but much smaller and yellow bill eliminates all except Alpine Chough (which has bright red legs). See Blue Rock Thrush and Ring Ouzel for differences from those species. Female is darker than Song Thrush and Mistle Thrush, particularly on unspotted underparts.

▽ Adult male   ▽ Adult female

SONG THRUSH *Turdus philomelos* 21cm

Fairly common resident in northern third of Spain, but scarce (and present only in uplands) in central regions. Widespread and abundant in winter, when immigrants increase populations. The archetypal thrush, with thickly spotted white underparts and brown upperparts. Very similar to Mistle Thrush, but markedly smaller and shyer, and less pot-bellied. Close examination reveals a uniform face with a bold eye-ring (blotchy on Mistle), and spots on underparts that are heart-shaped (almost broad-based bars on Mistle). Flies lower and with more urgency than Mistle, typically darting into deep cover rather than posing in treetops. Underwing also differs noticeably: yellow-orange on Song but contrastingly white on Mistle.

REDWING *Turdus iliacus* 21cm

Near Threatened. Winter visitor throughout Spain, but most common in the northern third. In the south, most frequent above 1,300m. Gregarious. Similar in size to Song Thrush, and – being essentially small and dark – can be hard to tell apart in brief flight views. However, Redwing's obvious broad cream stripe above eye is unique among Spanish thrushes, as are its rusty flanks and underwing. Flocks call routinely, particularly at night (a classic late-autumn sound, as birds migrate overhead): a thin, high, plaintive *tsiii.*

MISTLE THRUSH *Turdus viscivorus* 27cm

Common resident throughout most of Spain. Favours woodland, parkland and hedgerows; rarer in cities and shuns arid, treeless areas. Big, bold thrush of open areas, where it hops along confidently. Often moves in family groups, flying high with powerful, stuttering wingbeats. Most similar in plumage to smaller Song Thrush (for differences, see that species). Female paler and spottier than female Common Blackbird (see that species). In flight, white underwing rules out all thrushes except similar-sized and much more colourful Fieldfare (*Turdus pilaris*; not illustrated, uncommon winter visitor to the north).

CETTI'S WARBLER *Cettia cetti* 13.5cm

Common resident throughout Spain, except in the Pyrenees and a few excessively arid areas. Occupies dense vegetation in wet habitats, reedbeds and scrubby thickets. Medium-sized, dumpy, dark warbler that skulks in dense vegetation, popping up into the open to sing, then flying low between patches of cover like a big Winter Wren with a long, rounded tail. More often heard than seen: song is a sudden, explosive outburst, rich and intense (unlike any other

reedbed sound); call is a sharp *chip*. Differs from Eurasian Reed Warbler by having dark chestnut upperparts, ashy underparts, strong pink legs and long, rounded tail. Broader, more rounded tail and short wings create a body shape quite unlike that of Common Nightingale, and further differentiated from that species by its sullied underparts and contrasting face pattern.

ZITTING CISTICOLA *Cisticola juncidis* 10cm

Fairly common resident, but unevenly distributed. Favours the Mediterranean coast, Andalucía and Extremadura; absent from forests, mountains and cold regions. Very small indeed, with wings and tail that are both short and rounded – creating a distinctive silhouette during characteristic long, bounding songflight (quite unlike any other Spanish bird). Song is less impressive: a metallic *tzik*, given in a long series, one per second. Heavily streaked upperparts could prompt confusion with pipits (*Anthus* spp.), but smaller, with plain buff underparts and an open facial expression, and rarely (if ever) on the ground. Sedge Warbler (*Acrocephalus schoenobaenus*; not illustrated, passage migrant across Spain) also streaked above, but has a broad white stripe above eye and lacks Zitting Cisticola's white band on tail-tip.

COMMON GRASSHOPPER WARBLER *Locustella naevia* 13cm

Uncommon summer visitor to northernmost Spain, along the coast west of the Pyrenees. Common but overlooked passage migrant. Frequents damp scrub, wet meadows with dense vegetation, and bushy reedbeds. Secretive, creeping through undergrowth; typically located when singing, when it often perches in the open. Song is distinctive – a mechanical, reeling trill for several minutes, sounding more like a cicada than a bird. Streaked back eliminates Eurasian Reed Warbler. Lacks bold white stripe above eye of Sedge Warbler (*Acrocephalus schoenobaenus*; not illustrated, widespread on passage). Larger than Zitting Cisticola, with dark (not pale) face and longer tail that lacks white tips. Beware effect of light, which varies coloration from pale yellow-brown to dark, rusty brown.

WESTERN OLIVACEOUS WARBLER *Iduna opaca* 13cm

Also called Isabelline Warbler. Scarce summer visitor that is locally distributed in the south and east. Favours open woodland, parks and orchards, particularly in river valleys. Fairly large, slim and long-tailed warbler with nondescript sandy-brown upperparts and off-white underparts. Plumage duller than Eurasian Reed Warbler, and with a heavier bill and – importantly – square-ended (rather than rounded) tail-tip. Dull tones also differentiate Western Olivaceous from adult Melodious Warbler (which has yellow and green tones). Harder to distinguish from immature Melodious, although latter usually has lemony tones to breast and face, and olive shade to upperparts.

MELODIOUS WARBLER *Hippolais polyglotta* 13cm

Common summer visitor, breeding throughout Spain except in treeless terrain or mountains. Favours bushes, scrub and hedgerows. Breeding adult's olive-and-yellow coloration may prompt confusion with Willow Warbler. Chunkier, slower-moving and more skulking than that species, with rear crown feathers regularly raised (particularly when singing) and indistinct supercilium (stripe above eye) rather than Willow's broad supercilium. Breeding adult's coloration separates it from brown-and-white Eurasian Reed Warbler. However, first-winter and non-breeding adult Melodious are greyish and more likely to be confused with Eurasian Reed – look for Melodious's plain face (eye more prominent) and longer, pinker bill. To distinguish from Western Olivaceous Warbler, see that species.

▲ Adult male   ▲ Juvenile

EURASIAN REED WARBLER   *Acrocephalus scirpaceus*   13cm

Common and widespread summer visitor. Absent from mountains; most common in river valleys. Very common on passage. Breeds in damp reedbeds, but frequents drier habitats, including bushes, on migration. Often ascends a tall reed stem to sing, moving head from side to side with white throat puffed out. Weak stripe over eye, white eye-ring and longer bill differentiate it from larger, stockier but equally plain Garden Warbler. Garden shuns reedbeds, but both species skulk in scrub on migration. Unstreaked back and white throat could prompt confusion with female/first-winter Common Whitethroat, but latter is larger, with a stubbier bill and white sides to long tail.

GREAT REED WARBLER   *Acrocephalus arundinaceus*   18cm

Relatively common summer visitor, particularly in the east and south. Scarce in the north and absent from uplands. More localised than Eurasian Reed Warbler, with which it shares the habitat of tall reedbeds. As name suggests, Great Reed Warbler recalls a very large version of Eurasian Reed, being noticeably chunky, with a large head, broad tail and hefty bill. Often crashes about reeds, whereas Eurasian Reed moves deftly and unobtrusively. Singing male raises crest and puffs out white throat. Song loud and coarser than that of Eurasian Reed: deeper, harsher and more repetitive.

▽ Adult male   ▽ Adult

BALEARIC WARBLER *Sylvia balearica* 13cm

Endemic to the Balearics, where it is a very common resident across much of Mallorca, Cabrera, Ibiza and Formentera, although now extinct on Menorca. Absent from mainland Spain. Until recently, Balearic Warbler was considered the same species as Marmora's Warbler (*Sylvia sarda*; not illustrated) of Corsica and Sardinia. Inhabits low maquis and *garrigue*, plus rocky coastal scrub. Closely resembles Dartford Warbler, which is the only real confusion species, both being particularly small, long-tailed, punk-headed, all-dark and skulking *Sylvia* warblers. Adult Balearic differs from Dartford in having wholly grey underparts with, at best, a slight pinkish hue to flanks. In contrast, Dartford's underparts are a vigorous reddish pink (male) or dull pink-brown (female).

DARTFORD WARBLER *Sylvia undata* 13cm

Near Threatened. Very common resident, although absent from intensively cultivated areas. It has recently colonised the Balearics (where it could be confused with Balearic Warbler; see that species for differences). A distinctively dark, long-tailed bird that typically skulks in dense vegetation of dry, scrubby habitats such as heathland, *garrigue* and open maquis. Dark underparts rule out confusion with pale-bellied Common Whitethroat and Lesser Whitethroat (*Sylvia curruca*; not illustrated, rare autumn migrant, particularly in the east). Male's russet-brown underparts (left) could prompt confusion with male Subalpine Warbler, but brick-red coloration and white moustachial stripe of that species should be noticeable in a good view.

▲ Adult male

▲ Adult female

SPECTACLED WARBLER *Sylvia conspicillata* 12.5cm

Uncommon summer visitor to the southern two-thirds of Spain, and a few may winter in the south-east. Favours arid vegetation such as scrubby, low *garrigue*. Smaller version of the widespread Common Whitethroat. Male differs from that species in its big-headed and more colourful appearance, with a darker, blue-grey head, particularly in front of eye, contrasting with broad white eye-ring ('spectacles'). Neat white throat stands out against dusky pink underparts; Common Whitethroat looks insipid in comparison. Females of both species are very similar, but can be differentiated by size; Spectacled also has a more striking chestnut wing. See Subalpine Warbler for differences from that species.

SUBALPINE WARBLER *Sylvia cantillans* 12cm

Common summer visitor to much of Spain, although absent from the south-west, Cantabria and the Pyrenees. Skulks in low, bushy scrub – maquis, *garrigue* and hedgerows. Male is a particularly attractive warbler, with brick-red underparts and grey-blue upperparts separated by a white moustachial stripe. Red eye and underpart coloration distinguish it from male Spectacled Warbler. Females and first-winters are trickier to separate, but Subalpine tends to have a brown (rather than chestnut) wing and a ghosting of male's underpart pattern. Latter feature also differentiates them from female Common Whitethroat.

▼ Adult male

▼ Adult female

▲ Adult male   ▲ Adult female

SARDINIAN WARBLER *Sylvia melanocephala* 13.5cm

Very common resident throughout Spain except most of the north-western quadrant; particularly abundant in the east and south, and in the Balearics. Skulks in undergrowth, scrub and gardens. Slightly smaller than Common Whitethroat. On a good view (when not hiding in vegetation), Sardinian is distinctive. Male's black head contrasts with bright red eye/eye-ring and white throat – a combination shown by no other Spanish warbler. Lesser Whitethroat (*Sylvia curruca*; not illustrated, rare autumn migrant, particularly in the east) has a grey head and eye is not red. Male Eurasian Blackcap has a grey throat and also lacks red eye. Female Sardinian's red eye and eye-ring (and darker plumage) distinguish it from female Subalpine Warbler.

WESTERN ORPHEAN WARBLER *Sylvia hortensis* 15cm

Uncommon summer visitor to most of Spain, and absent from the far north and deforested regions. Favours low, open Mediterranean woodland, including olive groves. Markedly larger, heftier and stronger-billed than Eurasian Blackcap, with slow, deliberate movements. Differs from other Spanish *Sylvia* warblers in its startling white iris, which is particularly obvious in the adult male as it contrasts with the blackish hood. Additionally differs from male Sardinian Warbler in brown (rather than grey) back and buff (not grey) underparts.

▲ Adult male   ▲ Juvenile

COMMON WHITETHROAT *Sylvia communis* 14cm

Fairly common summer visitor, mainly to northern Spain and mountains elsewhere. Absent from arid zones. Very common on passage. Inhabits scrub with dense undergrowth in a variety of open-country habitats. Large warbler, bright and perky, and less skulking than other *Sylvia* species. Male often seen in songflight before dropping to perch. Chestnut patch on wing is common to all plumages, and rules out all similar species except Spectacled Warbler (for differences, see that species). For differences from Eurasian Reed Warbler, Dartford Warbler, Subalpine Warbler and Sardinian Warbler, see those species. Larger and browner than Lesser Whitethroat (*Sylvia curruca*; not illustrated, rare autumn migrant, particularly in the east), which is a clean grey and white.

GARDEN WARBLER *Sylvia borin* 14cm

Common summer visitor to northern Spain, plus pockets in the central mountains and east. Very common on migration. A bird of woodland and parks with decent undergrowth. Nondescript brown warbler with no obvious distinguishing features; indeed, its very blandness is the best way to recognise it. Lacks black or chestnut cap of similar-sized Eurasian Blackcap. Spotted Flycatcher is also grey-brown, but perches vertically and has a streaked breast on white underparts. Lacks white underparts of Eurasian Reed Warbler and has a very prominent black eye in otherwise plain face (rather than a pale line above eye and eye-ring). Common Whitethroat is longer-tailed, with (in all plumages) extensively chestnut wings and a white throat.

▲ Adult male   ▲ Adult female

EURASIAN BLACKCAP   *Sylvia atricapilla*   14cm

Common resident throughout most of Spain, particularly in the north and in damp mountains. More local in the south, and absent from treeless regions. Numbers are supplemented by wintering birds from elsewhere in Europe and by passage migrants. Inhabits woodland, parks and gardens with dense undergrowth. Stocky, rather lethargic warbler. Nondescript brown above and grey below. Striking feature – unique among warblers – is the neat skullcap: black in male, chestnut in female. Male Sardinian Warbler has a more extensive black head, contrasting with red eye and white throat. On plumage, male Eurasian Blackcap is confusable with Marsh Tit. That species is smaller and shorter-tailed, however, with black on head extending to nape, in front of eyes and chin, and with whiter cheeks and underparts.

WESTERN BONELLI'S WARBLER   *Phylloscopus bonelli*   11cm

Common and widespread summer visitor, but unevenly distributed. Absent from parts of Galicia and Cantabria; in the south, favours mountains. Prefers warm, fairly dry woodlands – whether deciduous or evergreen. *Phylloscopus* warblers are small, active, pale birds that usually forage high in trees. Western Bonelli's differs from other Spanish members of its genus in being relatively plain-faced (with a less prominent pale stripe above the eye), with bright yellow-green wings and tail contrasting with markedly dull grey-olive upperparts. Adult is particularly vibrant (although never as clean-cut as Wood Warbler, *Phylloscopus sibilatrix*; not illustrated, rare breeder and scarce migrant), but first-winter is duller, prompting confusion with Common Chiffchaff. Song is a soft, bubbling trill, similar to that of Wood. Call is a loud, disyllabic *tu-iii*, recalling Common Redstart.

COMMON CHIFFCHAFF *Phylloscopus collybita* 11cm

Fairly common resident breeder in the Pyrenees, Cataluña and scattered areas in the north. In winter and on migration, occurs abundantly throughout Spain, particularly in the south. Inhabits any wooded or scrubby landscape provided it has a dense undergrowth for nesting. The most drab Spanish *Phylloscopus* warbler, being a fairly nondescript grey-olive above and dingy whitish below; Willow Warbler is typically yellower. Uniquely among close relatives, it has black legs (rather than pink/brown), so focus attention on these. Also regularly dips its tail – unlike other members of the genus. Song is a distinctive, simple, two-toned *chip-chap*, woven into a long series. Also attracts attention with soft *hoo-it* call.

IBERIAN CHIFFCHAFF *Phylloscopus ibericus* 11cm

Fairly common summer visitor, most frequent in Galicia and Cantabria, with isolated populations in the south (Sierra Morena and mountains around Cádiz). Favours mixed and deciduous woodland, often along rivers. Until recently, considered the same species as Common Chiffchaff and hard to tell apart unless vocalising. Call is a soft, disyllabic, downslurred *wiii-ooo*. Song starts similarly to that of Common, then includes a stammering phrase before finishing with long whistles. Appearance *very* similar to Common, Iberian is slightly longer-winged, with a paler bill and brown (rather than black) legs. It has yellower plumage overall (rather like Willow Warbler), particularly on throat and vent, and a weaker eye-ring than Common.

WILLOW WARBLER *Phylloscopus trochilus* 11.5cm

Abundant passage migrant, but only a few pairs stay to breed in north and north-east Spain. Frequents woodlands, young conifer plantations and shrubby areas with scattered trees – although passage migrants may use other habitats. An olive-yellow warbler with a prominent pale stripe over the eye. Best known for its song (spring migrants may sing): a luscious, descending cadence. Very similar to Common Chiffchaff (for differences, see that species). Less bright and crisp than Western Bonelli's Warbler, and lacking that species' bright yellow-green fringing to wings and tail.

GOLDCREST *Regulus regulus* 9cm

Fairly common breeder, but restricted to the Pyrenees, Cantabrian mountains and upland pine forests of the central region. More common and widespread in winter, when it moves beyond woodland to occupy scrub and parks, but still absent from southern Spain. Europe's joint smallest bird (with Common Firecrest) and thus easy to recognise. Shape is that of a small, thick-necked, short-tailed *Phylloscopus* warbler. Immediately separable from common Spanish members of that genus by its well-marked wings (with a black square and two white bars), and black-and-yellow crown-stripes on otherwise plain face (lacks pale stripe above eye, as in warblers). Often heard before it is seen: call is a shrill, high-pitched *ssee-ssee-ssee*. See Common Firecrest for differences from that species.

COMMON FIRECREST *Regulus ignicapilla* 9cm

Widespread resident in northern Spain and in montane forest enclaves further south. More widespread in winter, when residents descending to lower altitudes are supplemented by immigrants from central Europe, and occupy a broader range of vegetated habitats. Tiny: size of Goldcrest. Much brighter than that species, with a vivid green back that turns bronze on shoulders, contrasting white underparts (usually gleaming in shady woodland) and a very bold, contrasting black-and-white face pattern. Latter much bolder than in Spanish warblers of the genus *Phylloscopus*, and with a bright yellow or orange central crown-stripe. Warblers are also larger and lack black-and-white pattern on wings.

SPOTTED FLYCATCHER *Muscicapa striata* 14cm

Generally a common summer visitor, but irregularly distributed. Most likely to be seen in the north and along the Mediterranean coast; scarce inland and in the north-west. Also a common, widespread passage migrant. Needs habitat that combines large trees and sunny, open areas. Flycatchers sit upright on bare branches, sallying out to catch prey. Spotted Flycatcher is the size of Common Chaffinch, but slimmer and with a vertical posture. Dull brown bird, differing from the similarly nondescript Garden Warbler in its posture, streaked underparts, white dots on wing and active flycatching behaviour.

 Adult male   ▲ Adult female

EUROPEAN PIED FLYCATCHER *Ficedula hypoleuca* 13cm

Fairly common but localised summer visitor, particularly favouring montane forests in the north. Also a common passage migrant, particularly in the west in autumn and the east in spring. Smaller and more compact than Spotted Flycatcher and more strikingly patterned. Male is very distinctive: no other Spanish landbird has its pattern of black upperparts, bold white wing-flash, white droplet on forehead and white underparts. Female is dowdier, but easily distinguished from Spotted Flycatcher by dint of extensive white in wing and unstreaked underparts.

LONG-TAILED TIT *Aegithalos caudatus* 14cm

Common, widespread resident throughout most of Spain. Most numerous in the north and in central Spain. Absent from the south-west, and restricted to montane forests elsewhere in the south. Uses a variety of bushy, wooded habitats from gardens to forests, and inhabits both rural areas and towns. An unmistakable tiny bird, whose elongated tail accounts for almost two-thirds of its length. Only Bearded Reedling (*Panurus biarmicus*; not illustrated, scarce and localised resident of reedbeds) has proportions even vaguely similar; its basic coloration (sandy, not black and white) and habitat (reedbeds) eliminate confusion. In addition to tail length, head pattern (largely white, with a broad black 'bushy eyebrow') eliminates confusion with Coal Tit (which has a largely black head with a white cheek and central crown-stripe). Parties roll through habitats, staying in contact with a distinctive rolling *brrp* trill.

MARSH TIT *Poecile palustris* 12cm

Very common resident in northern Spain, but restricted to upland pine forests in the centre and east of the country. Favours habitats with old trees (including parks and gardens). Small tit with brown upperparts and a distinct black cap. This combination of colour rules out other tits bar Coal Tit. Differs from latter in large size, wholly black cap (lacking white stripe on nape), brown (not grey) upperparts and lack of white bands on wing. Could be mistaken for male Eurasian Blackcap (for differences, see that species). First clue to its presence (and identification) is often its distinctive call: a cheery, emphatic *pit-chew*.

EUROPEAN CRESTED TIT *Lophophranes cristatus* 11.5cm

Common resident but erratically distributed. Restricted to pine forests, so most common in the north. Scarce in the arid south-east; absent from the Balearics. Enters parks and gardens (with pine trees), albeit mainly in winter. Jaunty tit, its perky demeanour accentuated by its most distinctive plumage feature: a tall black-and-white crest. This 'headgear' differentiates it from all other Spanish birds. If crest is not visible (perhaps when bird is high in a tree), striking cheek pattern (a black 'C' on a white face) and black collar joining up with black throat are diagnostic. Birds are often first detected by their call: a unique purring trill.

COAL TIT *Periparus ater* 11cm

Scarce resident of humid montane forests in extreme northern Spain, particularly where there are conifers. Frequents gardens and parks, particularly in winter, but is nervous of other birds – occupying the lowest rung in the tit pecking order! Spain's smallest tit, not much bigger than Goldcrest. In a brief view of a bird closeted in pines, double band on wing and general coloration may prompt thought of Goldcrest. When bird emerges, however, its diagnostic head pattern is obvious: black head with white cheeks and white stripe on nape. No other Spanish tit has such plumage.

EURASIAN BLUE TIT *Cyanistes caeruleus* 12cm

Very common throughout Spain, occurring in any habitat with trees or bushes – including urban gardens. Local, however, in the south-west and in treeless terrain. Winter populations are sometimes boosted by influxes of northern birds. Familiar and confiding bird, often announcing its presence with a cheery trill. Brightly coloured plumage more like that of a tropical rainforest bird than a Spanish species, and confusable only with Great Tit. Differs from latter in being small and having a whiter face with a dark line through eye, a blue (not black) cap and strikingly blue (not grey) wings. Yellow underparts and head pattern differentiate it from all other tits.

GREAT TIT *Parus major* 14cm

Very common resident throughout Spain, with winter numbers supplemented by arrivals from the north. Occurs wherever there are trees or bushes. Familiar bird, often frequenting gardens. Spain's largest tit, with distinctive plumage (particularly the yellow underparts) that minimises confusion with any bird except Eurasian Blue Tit (for differences, see that species) and Coal Tit. Head pattern similar to latter, but Great Tit lacks Coal's white nape. Brighter overall than Coal, with a green back (rather than grey) and yellow underparts (rather than sullied buff). Has a varied vocal repertoire (mystery calls often transpire to be Great Tits), most famously a see-sawing *teach-er*.

EURASIAN NUTHATCH *Sitta europaea* 14cm

Common resident in montane forests of the Pyrenees and Cantabria, uncommon in scattered locations elsewhere. Absent from arid or treeless terrain. Frequents woodland, particularly in cool, damp areas. Strictly arboreal, climbing up and down trunks and along branches – except when feeding on bird tables. Size of a Great Tit, but stockier, with a shorter tail and longer head and bill. Uniquely pale blue-grey above and warm buff below. Most striking feature is long black mask running from behind ear-coverts through eye (leading into long, pointed grey-black bill), which sits between blue-grey crown and white cheeks. Call is a distinctive, abrupt *chwit*; song is a nasal, ringing (almost whinnying) *twee-twee-twee*.

▲ Adult female

▲ Adult male

WALLCREEPER *Tichodroma muraria* 16cm

Scarce breeder in mountains of the central Pyrenees and Picos de Europa. May winter at lower altitudes, thus becoming more widespread; most likely in eastern Spain but remaining rare. In summer, strictly on rocks and cliff faces; in winter, sometimes on buildings or other structures such as bridges. Uniquely among Spanish birds, climbs up vertical rocky surfaces and swoops between them in butterfly-like flight on rounded wings. Unmistakable appearance – like a colourful treecreeper. In flight, crimson-and-black pattern on wings grabs attention. Harder to spot when climbing, as plumage is basically grey, black and white, but occasionally flashes or holds open wings, revealing its presence.

SHORT-TOED TREECREEPER *Certhia brachydactyla* 13cm

Very common resident throughout Spain, although absent from arid or treeless terrain. Favours broadleaved woodlands, parks and gardens, but most common in dense, mature forests in damp regions. Typical behaviour (spiralling up tree trunks) means it is likely to be confused only with Eurasian Treecreeper (*Certhia familiaris*; not illustrated), with which it overlaps in the montane forests of extreme northern Spain. Voice is the easiest way to tell this extremely similar pair apart: call is a penetrating, oft-repeated *tuut*, like that of Coal Tit. Identification by plumage involves careful examination of the exact pattern of the buff 'V' midway along the wing – a fairly neat line in Short-toed rather than the zigzag of Eurasian.

EURASIAN PENDULINE TIT   *Remiz pendulinus*   11cm

Uncommon and locally distributed resident, frequent only in the Ebro Valley. Numbers are boosted in winter by immigrants from central Europe. Favours wetlands, reedbeds and ditches, particularly with reedmace and usually with scattered trees for breeding. Smaller than Eurasian Blue Tit, with a tiny conical bill. Plumage distinctive, confusable only with much larger Red-backed Shrike. Male more striking than female, with broader black mask that, along with short tail, eliminates confusion with Bearded Reedling (*Panurus biarmicus*; not illustrated, scarce and localised resident of reedbeds). Juvenile dull brown, and could be confused with juvenile Bearded Reedling; Penduline's short tail sets things straight. Often located by its call: a drawn-out *pss-eee-oooo*, like the plaintive call of a Common Reed Bunting.

EURASIAN GOLDEN ORIOLE   *Oriolus oriolus*   24cm

Fairly common and widespread summer visitor to mature deciduous forest in lowland Spain. Most frequent in central-west Spain, and scarce in the north and in uplands. Scarce on passage in the Balearics. Size of Common Blackbird and brightly coloured – but don't expect those characteristics to make it easy to see! Habitually hides in dense, leafy canopy, attracting attention either by song (a rich, fluty whistling) or in sudden flight on surprisingly long wings. Adult male unmistakable, being golden yellow with almost entirely black wings and tail. Female more subdued, basically green but with darker wings and yellow on flanks and vent. Superficially similar to European Green Woodpecker, especially in flight, but has a shorter tail, contrastingly dark wings and a shorter pinkish-red bill.

▽ *Adult male*   ▽ *Adult female*

▲ Adult male ▲ Adult female

RED-BACKED SHRIKE *Lanius collurio* 17cm

Common summer visitor to northern Spain. Most frequent in mountains of Cantabria and the Pyrenees, although rare in Galicia. Spreading southwards. Frequents scrubby, semi-open environments. Shrikes are medium-sized songbirds with a dark eye-mask and hooked bill. They hunt from prominent perches and store a 'larder' of victims. Male Red-backed Shrike is distinctive, with a blue-grey crown and nape contrasting with chestnut back and wings, and a black eye-mask. Upperpart colour differentiates it from Southern Grey Shrike and male Northern Wheatear (which also lacks hooked bill and has a largely white tail). Female and first-winter resemble first-winter Woodchat Shrike (for differences, see that species).

SOUTHERN GREY SHRIKE *Lanius meridionalis* 24cm

Vulnerable. Fairly common but declining resident, now considered globally threatened. Most abundant in central and south-west Spain. Favours open environments with scattered trees and bushes. A shy bird that quickly retreats to cover before you can get close. This is a large grey shrike, with a particularly long, mainly black tail. Its plain grey back rules out both Red-backed Shrike and Woodchat Shrike, while white patches in the wing also eliminate the former. Superficially similar to much smaller Northern Wheatear, but has long, largely black tail, white in wing and a hooked bill.

▲ Adult male

▲ Juvenile

WOODCHAT SHRIKE *Lanius senator* 18cm

Common but declining summer visitor. Widespread: most abundant in the south and south-west, but absent from the extreme north. Passage migrants may be encountered anywhere in spring. Adult distinctive: the only black-and-white shrike with a russet cap. Female looks scruffier than male. First-winter resembles female/first-winter Red-backed Shrike, but Woodchat is a colder grey (rather than warm brown) above, and much more heavily scalloped. Also has a barred whitish (not brown) rump and more white on shoulders (a ghosting of adult's pattern).

EURASIAN JAY *Garrulus glandarius* 34cm

Resident in Spain, common in the north and in montane forests; absent in arid, treeless habitat. Frequents any wooded habitat, including urban gardens. Crows and jays are large, bulky birds with a strong bill. Eurasian Jay is distinctive, appearing largely pink at rest. Identity is not so obvious in flight, but look for the electric-blue flash on black-and-white wings, and neat white rump contrasting with wholly black tail. For differences from Azure-winged Magpie, see that species. When airborne, could be confused with Hoopoe, but latter has black-and-white stripes all the way across its back and wings, and a banded tail. Distinctive call: a harsh, screeching jeer.

▲ Adult   ▲ Juvenile

AZURE-WINGED MAGPIE *Cyanopica cyanus* 33cm

Common resident of Extremadura and surroundings, where it favours lightly wooded terrain. Alert, shy and gregarious outside the breeding season, foraging actively in treetops. Size of a Eurasian Jay, although half of its length comprises the tail. Overall shape is like that of a Common Magpie. Unmistakable; although pink plumage prompts thought of Eurasian Jay, long and extensively blue wings rule out that species. In shady vegetation, however, intensity of coloration can dissipate and cause momentary confusion.

COMMON MAGPIE *Pica pica* 45cm

Very common throughout most of Spain, being absent only from much of Andalucía and spots in the south-east. Frequents most open-country environments as long as they contain trees, although shuns closed-canopy woodland. Increasingly abundant near human habitation. Distinctive black-and-white crow with a tail that is as long as its body. Plumage is effectively black (shining blue, green or purple), bar white belly, shoulder-patches and (in flight) wing-tips. Only confusion might be with a partially leucistic (white) crow, but long tail should set the story straight. Clearly much larger and blacker than similarly long-tailed, black-and-white White Wagtail, which walks along the ground pumping its tail.

▲ Adult   ▲ Adult in flight

ALPINE CHOUGH *Pyrrhocorax graculus* 38cm

Fairly common resident in montane regions of the Pyrenees and Cantabria – usually well above 1,000m in alpine meadows and on sheer cliffs. Often congregates around ski resorts and restaurants. Some local dispersal in winter, when birds are more widespread and tolerant of lower altitudes. Choughs are acrobatic crows, sailing buoyantly around cliff faces before plummeting downwards on half-folded wings. Alpine Chough is a small crow with a yellow bill and red legs. Most similar to Red-billed Chough (for differences, see that species). Yellow bill and all-black plumage could lead to confusion with male Common Blackbird, but latter is much smaller, and has a brighter yellow bill and pink-brown (not red) legs.

RED-BILLED CHOUGH *Pyrrhocorax pyrrhocorax* 39cm

Uncommon, sparsely distributed resident in mountainous regions of much of eastern Spain. Alpine Chough is the most likely confusion species; even then, it will provoke uncertainty only if Red-billed's eponymous decurved scarlet bill cannot be seen. Red-billed looks a glossier black than Alpine, and longer-bodied. In flight, its wing-tips are more prominently 'fingered' (rounded on Alpine). Red bill and legs remove confusion with other all-black crows (such as Western Jackdaw, which can also fly acrobatically, high in the sky) and with smaller male Common Blackbird. Call is striking: a long, nasal *chiiiaooow*.

▲ Adult male

▲ Adult in flight

WESTERN JACKDAW *Corvus monedula* 32cm

Common resident throughout most of Spain, but scarce or absent from northern coasts and declining in Cataluña. Uses a wide range of open habitats, particularly farmland, as long as there are buildings or trees for nesting. Compact crow, roughly the size of Eurasian Jay. Differs from Carrion Crow in its smaller size, staring white (or very pale blue) iris and pale grey shawl on neck. In flight, looks much smaller than that species, with quicker, flickering wingbeats. Flocks often swirl out from trees, particularly before roosting, sailing around lazily before returning to perch. Voice distinctive: a metallic, abrupt, resonant *jak*.

CARRION CROW *Corvus corone* 47cm

Common resident in northern and eastern Spain, frequenting any open environment, including urban areas and alpine meadows. Absent in most of the south. Large black bird – larger than Western Jackdaw. Often solitary but occasionally gathers in flocks. Most similar to larger Northern Raven (for differences, see that species). Similar also to Rook (*Corvus frugilegus*; not illustrated), but distribution means confusion is unlikely (Rook is a scarce resident in León only). In addition, Carrion Crow has a shorter, less tapered bill with black skin (not white) at its base, and in flight looks less ragged, with a shorter tail, less angled wings and less protruding head. Call is a hoarse *kraaa*.

▽ Adult

▽ Adult in flight

▲ Adults   ▲ Adult in flight

NORTHERN RAVEN *Corvus corax* **61cm**

Fairly common resident across Spain, with the exception of flat lowlands and treeless regions. Most frequent in rocky mountains. Massive black crow, the size of Common Buzzard. Carrion Crow is the only confusion species, but it is smaller and less extravagantly shaped. Northern Raven has a distinctive form in flight, with a long diamond-shaped tail (rounded in other crows), thick neck and powerful yet laid-back beats of often-angled wings. At rest, its bulk is apparent, being complemented by a heavy, steeply arched bill. Call is distinctive: a far-carrying *tonk* or *prruk*.

SPOTLESS STARLING *Sturnus unicolor* **22cm**

Very common and gregarious resident throughout Spain, favouring open regions but also frequenting urban areas. For most of the year, in all bar northern and parts of eastern Spain, this is the country's only starling species. In winter, however, Common Starling also occurs throughout Spain. At this season, the two species need careful differentiation, because Spotless Starling betrays its name by being slightly spotted! The pale dots are, however, much smaller than those of Common, and are usually absent from the crown and mantle (where Common is always spotted). In addition, Spotless never shows Common's brown fringing to wings, and often has obviously bright pink legs. Moreover, any sheen is more likely to be solely purple compared to the various iridescent tones exhibited by Common. In summer, differences are more marked: Common is spotty, whereas Spotless is an unmarked purplish black.

COMMON STARLING *Sturnus vulgaris* 22cm

Common (and spreading) resident in northern and north-eastern Spain, and an abundant winter visitor elsewhere. Occupies many open environments, including urban areas. Gregarious, forming large flocks, particularly in winter, when pre-roost murmurations can be spectacular. Particularly in winter, very similar to Spotless Starling (for differences, see that species). Both starlings are dark birds that can be confused with Common Blackbird, but are smaller and shorter-tailed, and walk along the ground rather than hopping. In flight, their wings are markedly triangular and thus very different from those of Common Blackbird.

HOUSE SPARROW *Passer domesticus* 15cm

Abundant resident throughout mainland Spain and the Balearics. Particularly common near human dwellings. Familiar species, attracting attention by chirping. Uniquely, male has a grey crown, chestnut band behind eye and a black bib. See Eurasian Tree Sparrow for differences from that species. Female House Sparrow lacks male's head pattern, bold white wing-band of female Common Chaffinch and streaked underparts of Corn Bunting; most similar to Rock Sparrow (for differences, see that species).

▽ *Adult male*

▽ *Adult female*

▲ Adult male   ▲ Adult female

SPANISH SPARROW *Passer hispaniolensis* 15cm

Common resident throughout much of Spain except in the north and mountains, from which it is absent. Densities vary markedly: most common in cultivated areas. Size of House Sparrow and larger than Eurasian Tree Sparrow. Breeding male Spanish very smart, differing from male House in black (not brown) back, more extensive black over most of underparts (rather than just bib, as on House), largely white face and russet-brown (not grey) cap. First two features also differentiate Spanish from both sexes of Eurasian Tree. Winter-plumaged male scruffier and more like House, but white cheeks and brown crown remain. Female House and Spanish sparrows are effectively identical; latter is sometimes more streaked on flanks and has a larger bill.

EURASIAN TREE SPARROW *Passer montanus* 14cm

Common resident throughout most of Spain, but absent from mountains (and thus from the Pyrenees and parts of Cantabria). Typically occurs close to human habitation in countryside – for example, in hedgerows near villages. Unlike House Sparrow, sexes do not differ in plumage. On a good view, easily distinguished from House by wholly chestnut-brown crown, large black spot on white cheek, and neat black chin not extending onto breast. Slightly smaller and more compact than House – a difference perceptible in flight, when it utters a distinctive, hard *tec*.

ROCK SPARROW *Petronia petronia* 16cm

Common and widespread resident in Spain, most frequent in the east.
Absent or very local in Cantabria and Galicia. Frequents open rocky
environments and stony grasslands. Stockier than House Sparrow,
with longer wings, a larger head, bigger bill and shorter tail, which
give it a very different silhouette, particularly in flight. At a distance,
plumage looks variegated, which should be the first clue that this is
not a female House. Closer examination reveals Rock Sparrow to have
a much more contrasting head pattern than female House – pale
crown-stripe, dark side to head and broad pale band above eye – and
heavily streaked underparts.

WHITE-WINGED SNOWFINCH *Montifringilla nivalis* 17cm

Scarce resident of rocky mountains above 2,000m in Picos de Europa
and the Pyrenees. In winter, occasionally descends to lower altitudes
and may be found around ski-resort restaurants. Large, long-winged
finch of mountain-tops. Nondescript grey and brown on the ground,
but in flight reveals diagnostic, startling white-and-black wings. No
real confusion species at this high altitude. On the ground, could be
confused with Alpine Accentor, which is also grey and brown, but
latter is heavily streaked and lacks white in wing. Accentor also looks
rather thrush-like in flight (when all-dark wings avoid confusion).

▲ Adult

▲ Juvenile

COMMON WAXBILL *Estrilda astrild* 11cm

Originally from Africa, but introduced to Portugal in the 1960s, from where it has spread into Extremadura and west Galicia. Now a gregarious, locally common resident. Favours damp vegetation such as rushes. Very small, finch-like bird with a long tail (unlike any Spanish finch) and chattering call. Red bill (hence the name waxbill, from sealing wax) means it is likely to be confused only with the female of another non-native member of the same family, Red Avadavat (see that species for differences).

RED AVADAVAT *Amandava amandava* 10cm

Originally from South Asia, but introduced to Spain in the 1970s or 1980s and now a common resident in Extremadura, parts of Andalucía and a few other places. Tiny; even smaller than Common Waxbill, with a similarly long tail. Red bill removes confusion with any other Spanish bird except Common Waxbill. Can be differentiated from that species in all plumages by white spots on black wings and eye-catching scarlet rump and uppertail-coverts. Breeding male dramatic, being largely bright red with white spots.

▽ Adult male, breeding plumage   ▽ Adult, non-breeding plumage

▲ *Adult male*   ▲ *Adult female*

COMMON CHAFFINCH *Fringilla coelebs* 15cm

Very common resident throughout Spain, with the exception of treeless or arid parts. In winter, numbers are increased by visitors from further north. Familiar finch, similar in size to House Sparrow but with a longer tail. Sexes are very different in plumage, but share a diagnostic pattern of broad white bands on wings. This striking feature, visible at rest and in flight, eliminates confusion with all other finches as well as sparrows. Brambling (*Fringilla montifringilla*; not illustrated, scarce winter visitor, particularly to the north) has a single white band on wing, but differs in its neat white rump and orange on forewing. Common Chaffinch calls are also characteristic – a cheery *pink* and a melancholy *hooo-it* – as is its accelerating rattle of a song.

EUROPEAN SERIN *Serinus serinus* 11cm

Abundant resident, particularly in the south. Favours open environments with tall trees, often in villages and parks. Tiny, streaky finch that attracts attention with its vocalisations (variations of jingling trills) and, in flight, its bright yellow rump. Latter differentiates it from the larger, greener, less streaky European Greenfinch. Male has a largely yellow face, including crown – thus separating it from male Eurasian Siskin (which has a black crown). Female is duller and densely streaked: differs from Common Linnet in yellow rump, and from female Eurasian Siskin in subdued (not contrastingly black-and-yellow) wing pattern. See Citril Finch for differences from that species.

▼ *Adult male*   ▼ *Adult female*

▲ Adult   ▲ Juvenile

CITRIL FINCH   *Serinus citrinella*   12cm

Locally common species of conifer forests and forest edges above
1,000m in northern and central Spain, notably Picos de Europa and
the Pyrenees. Some individuals winter at lower altitudes. Similar in size
and shape to Eurasian Siskin, but adults immediately differ from that
species (and from diminutive European Serin) by being only finely
streaked on back. European Greenfinch is similarly unstreaked but
much larger, and Citril Finch is further distinguished by grey shawl,
yellower underparts and yellow-green bars crossing wing (rather than
European Greenfinch's broad yellow streak along length of wing).
Habitat should also help: Citril is very much montane.

EUROPEAN GREENFINCH   *Carduelis chloris*   15cm

Very common resident throughout Spain, particularly in hot areas,
with numbers boosted in winter by northern migrants. Similar in size
to Common Chaffinch, but stockier and with a shorter tail and thicker
bill. All plumages are easily identifiable in flight, when bright yellow
streak along leading edge of outer wing catches the eye. No other
species shows such a pattern, so this is the quickest way to distinguish
juvenile European Greenfinch from other streaky finches such as
European Serin and Eurasian Siskin. In addition, male differs from all
other green finches in wholly pink bill. Song – a ringing, energetic trill
– is often given in songflight at treetop level.

▼ Adult male   ▼ Adult female

EUROPEAN GOLDFINCH *Carduelis carduelis* 12cm

Very common resident throughout Spain, with higher numbers in winter thanks to immigration from the north. Small, distinctive finch with an attractive, tinkling song. No real confusion species, as all plumages have a unique broad yellow band across wing, which is visible both at rest and in flight. Adult (above) further differs from all other Spanish birds in red face in front of eye contrasting with white cheeks and black crown/collar. Juvenile lacks this bold head pattern and could conceivably be overlooked among flocks of European Greenfinch or Common Linnet – until it takes flight. Often in family groups.

EURASIAN SISKIN *Carduelis spinus* 12cm

Scarce resident of montane forests in northern Spain, particularly in the Pyrenees. Better known as a widespread and occasionally very common winter visitor, particularly in the north and along the eastern coast. Small, slender greenish finch often seen feeding acrobatically in upper branches, keeping in contact with others by its plaintive, disyllabic *tlii-uu* call. Male is boldly patterned with black, yellow, green and white. Female and first-winter are paler, greyer and streakier, with isolated patches of yellow. For differences from European Serin, Citril Finch and European Greenfinch, see those species.

▼ *Adult male*

▼ *Adult female*

▲ Adult male   ▲ Adult female

COMMON LINNET *Carduelis cannabina* 13cm

Very common resident throughout Spain, particularly abundant in warmer areas. In the east, particularly prominent in winter and on passage. Gregarious finch, often flocking with other species. Constantly active: rarely settles for long before bounding into the air, twittering, then dropping back down to low vegetation. In flight, look for white flashes in wing and tail. At rest, male is easily identifiable by pink breast/forehead and unstreaked chestnut back. Female and first-winter are less distinctive, being drab grey-brown and streaky, and could be confused with juvenile Citril Finch. Latter, however, always has yellow tones to plumage and yellowish wing-bars, and lacks white flashes in Common Linnet's wing.

RED CROSSBILL *Loxia curvirostra* 16cm

Uncommon resident in extensive conifer forests in both mountains and lowlands, particularly in the east and north. Numbers vary between years, with nomadic movements within and into the country. Very rarely seen away from pines. Big, stocky, large-headed finch with a short tail. At rest, diagnostic bill shape should be visible: strongly arched, with crossed tips. Usually seen in groups that maintain contact in rapid, purposeful flight with a ringing *jip-jip-jip*. Plumage varies from greyish green (juvenile and female) to dull scarlet (adult male), but lacks any contrasting white or yellow patches (as on European Greenfinch). Combination of shape, bill structure, habitat and plumage makes Red Crossbills easy to identify, given a good view.

▽ Adult male   ▽ Adult female

EURASIAN BULLFINCH *Pyrrhula pyrrhula* 16cm

Uncommon resident in northernmost Spain, but patchily distributed. More widespread in winter, but still generally scarce. Surprisingly unobtrusive for such a boldly patterned bird, favouring dense vegetation in open woodland, scrubby forests and parkland. First sign of its presence is often a mournful, descending *peeoo* whistle. Striking, simply plumaged bird ('colour by numbers'). Sexes share a black cap, wings and tail, contrasting with extensive white rump and pale wing-bar. No other Spanish bird has such a pattern. Male has a blue-grey back and pink underparts, female a brown-grey back and buff-grey underparts.

HAWFINCH *Coccothraustes coccothraustes* 17cm

Scarce resident, particularly in south-western and central Spain. More widespread in winter, particularly along the north-eastern coast. Inhabits mature broadleaved woodland, particularly beech (*Fagus sylvatica*) and open scrubland with tall trees; in some areas, also frequents parks and gardens. Large, handsome finch with a big head, thick bill and short tail. Often perches in treetops before flying rapidly and directly to feeding grounds. Usual flight call is a quiet *tik*, like that of European Robin. In flight, pattern of white is unique, comprising band on tail-tip, shoulder-patch and stripe along wing-tip. This eliminates superficially similar male Common Chaffinch. At rest, very distinctive, with no confusion species.

▼ Adult male   ▼ Adult female

 Adult male

▲ Adult female

YELLOWHAMMER *Emberiza citrinella* 16cm

Declining resident of humid countryside in extreme northern Spain. Slightly more widespread in winter. Large, slender bunting with a long tail and strong yellow tones to plumage. Male is unique in its largely canary-yellow head and rusty rump; lacks markedly stripy head of more common and widespread Cirl Bunting. Female very like female Cirl Bunting, but rump is chestnut (not olive-grey) and underparts have thick streaks (not fine). Female's yellow and rusty tones eliminate female Common Reed Bunting and Corn Bunting; latter is also larger, tubbier and thicker-billed.

CIRL BUNTING *Emberiza cirlus* 16cm

Common resident throughout much of Spain, particularly in the north; absent from, or only a winter visitor to, treeless regions of the south. Frequents semi-open environments with bushes and hedgerows, including agricultural land. Male has a distinctive head pattern comprising dark olive stripes (often looking black) on yellow face and olive chest-band. Pattern is much bolder and darker than in male Yellowhammer (for differences between females, see that species). Compared to male Rock Bunting, male Cirl has more stripes on clearly yellow (not blue-grey) face, and rufous streaks on flanks rather than unmarked chestnut belly. Song is an undistinguished thin trill, lacking Yellowhammer's emphatic tones.

▼ Adult male

▼ Adult female

▲ Adult male   ▲ Adult female

ROCK BUNTING   *Emberiza cia*   16cm

Common resident across much of Spain, particularly from mid-altitudes upwards, dispersing lower down in winter. Favours rocky areas with ample scrub and bushes. Male is particularly attractive, and female subdued in comparison (although basic plumage pattern is similar). Recalls male Cirl Bunting, but head is blue-grey rather than yellow and has fewer black stripes. Rump is rusty as in Yellowhammer and unlike olive-grey of Cirl. Uniquely among buntings, Rock's belly and flanks are unmarked chestnut.

ORTOLAN BUNTING   *Emberiza hortulana*   16cm

Uncommon and declining summer visitor with an irregular distribution concentrated on north-central Spain. Breeds in farmland, chalk grassland, and hedgerows in cultivated areas. Uses a variety of open environments on passage. Slender, pale bunting with a narrow pink bill and distinctive face on which a broad pale eye-ring stands out – a combination not seen in any other Spanish bunting. Male is pastel-coloured, having a pale green face with a yellow cheek-stripe and chin, and pale orange underparts. Female and first-winter are more washed out, but share the same face pattern.

▼ Adult female   ▼ Adult male, breeding plumage

COMMON REED BUNTING *Emberiza schoeniclus* 16cm

Rare local resident in northern Spain. More widespread in winter, when particularly common in the east. The most likely bunting to be seen in reedbeds (indeed, in wetlands full stop). Female (right) and first-winter are a mass of brown and buff stripes. Summer male is brighter, with a white stripe separating black head from black bib, and cleaner white underparts. Winter male has faded version of summer head pattern. No common Spanish bunting is even vaguely similar. On a poor view, female's broad pale stripe above eye and stripy back could prompt thought of a

Sedge Warbler (*Acrocephalus schoenobaenus*; not illustrated, passage migrant across Spain), but that species is much smaller and shorter-tailed, with plain underparts and a slender bill.

CORN BUNTING *Emberiza calandra* 18cm

Very common resident in most of Spain, but absent from mountains (and thus from much of Cantabria, Galicia and the Pyrenees). Very common in the Balearics. Favours lowland agricultural areas: crops, grassland, and ploughed fields with hedgerows. Large, streaked, plain brown bunting – much more nondescript than other Spanish buntings. Has a thicker bill than other buntings, lacks white sides to tail and sometimes flies with legs dangling. More likely to be confused with Eurasian Skylark, which frequents similar habitats but hops on the ground (rather than runs), and has an indistinct pale spot at back of cheeks and a much thicker, seed-eating bill. Distinctive song rendered as 'jangling of keys'.

▼ *Adult male*

▼ *Juvenile*

GLOSSARY

Bare parts A bird's unfeathered parts, including the bill, legs and feet, and sometimes the skin of the face.

Bib A patch of colour covering the throat and/or upper breast.

Breast-band A stripe of colour (usually dark) across the breast.

Call A simple sound made by a bird, usually for contact.

Carpal The 'elbow' of a bird's wing.

Collar A line or band, usually coloured, around the bottom of the neck.

Crest A tuft of feathers on top of a bird's head.

Decurved Curving downwards, as of the bill.

Drumming The repeated striking made by woodpeckers with their bill on a resonant tree branch or trunk; equivalent to song.

Ear-coverts The bird's cheek; often a discrete patch of colour.

Ear-tufts Tufts of feathers on either side of the top of a bird's head, as on some owls.

Eye-mask A patch of contrasting colour over the eye and upper ear-coverts.

Eye-ring A circle of coloured feathers or bare skin around the eye.

Eye-stripe A line of colour (usually dark) running from the bill to the eye and beyond.

First-winter A bird in the first-winter of its life. Often has a distinct plumage from that of adults.

Invertebrate Animals without a backbone, including insects, spiders, snails, etc.

Iridescent Exhibiting a brightly coloured sheen in certain light conditions.

Jizz The overall impression of a bird, garnered from its shape, structure and behaviour.

Leading edge The front edge of the opened wing, visible as the bird is flying.

Moustachial stripe A stripe (usually dark) running along the bottom edge of the ear-coverts.

Murmuration The (often spectacular) pre-roost flight of a flock of starlings.

Passage migrant A bird that occurs in a particular area only during its migratory journey, as it is passing through.

Primaries See 'wing-tip'.

Resident A bird that is present in a particular area year-round.

Scrub Habitats with plenty of bushes but few or no trees.

Secondaries The inner flight feathers on the rear of the wing.

Song The sound made by a bird (usually male) to advertise its territory; more complex than a call.

Songflight A type of flight performed as the bird sings.

Supercilium A stripe of colour (usually pale) above the eye, as if an 'eyebrow'.

Tail-band A stripe of colour across the tail, often the tail-tip.

Trailing edge The rear edge of the opened wing, visible as a bird flies.

Trousers The feathering on the lower belly that encases the legs of some perched birds, especially birds of prey.

Underparts The bottom side of a bird, usually including the chin, throat, breast, belly, flanks and vent.

Underwing The bottom side (underside) of a bird's wings.

Upperparts The top side of a bird, usually including the crown, neck, back and rump.

Upperwing The top side of a bird's wings.

Wing-bar or wing-stripe A stripe of contrasting colour on the wing. Sometimes visible when the bird is at rest, when the wing is folded; at other times visible only in flight, when the wing is spread.

Wing-tip The feathers at the very end of the bird's wing. Formally called the primaries.

RESORCES

BOOKS

de Juana, E. and Garcia, E. 2015. *Birds of the Iberian Peninsula.* Christopher Helm, London.

de Juana, E. and Varela, J. M. 2017. *Birds of Spain.* Lynx Edicions, Barcelona.

Farino, T. and Lockwood, M. 2003. *Travellers' Nature Guide: Spain.* Oxford University Press, Oxford.

Garcia, E. and Paterson, A. M. 2008. *Where to Watch Birds in Southern and Western Spain.* Christopher Helm, London.

Garcia, E. and Rebane, M. 2017. *Where to Watch Birds in Northern and Eastern Spain.* Christopher Helm, London.

Hilbers, D. 2013. *Extremadura, Spain.* Crossbill Guides, Arnhem.

Hilbers, D. and Woutersen. K. 2016. *Spanish Pyrenees and Steppes of Huesca, Spain.* Crossbill Guides, Arnhem.

Svensson, L., Mullarney, K. and Zetterström, D. 2009. *Collins Bird Guide.* 2nd edn. HarperCollins, London.

WEBSITES

www.seo.org
Website of the Sociedad Española de Ornitología (SEO/BirdLife), Spain's national bird conservation organisation; includes an online field guide to Spain's birds (effectively an Internet version of de Juana and Varela's 2017 *Birds of Spain*; see above) and information on good birdwatching locations.

www.cloudbirders.com
Cloud-based repository of birdwatching trip reports, including more than 1,500 from Spain.

www.rarebirdspain.net
Up-to-date information on vagrant birds in Spain.

SMARTPHONE APPS

These two smartphone apps enable you to enter your sightings in Spain (and around the world), and therefore contribute to the collective understanding of the status and distribution of birds. It's citizen science at its best.

eBird
http://tinyurl.com/ebirdapp

NaturaList
http://tinyurl.com/naturalistapp

137

ACKNOWLEDGEMENTS

Jenny Campbell (Bloomsbury) and Susi Bailey played invaluable roles during the book's production. James thanks Jim Martin (Bloomsbury) for commissioning the title, and Sharon and Maya Lowen for both granting him the time to write it and helping him explore Spain. He is grateful to Mike Hoit, Martin Kelsey and Will Soar for companionship on various birdwatching escapades in Spain, and to Matthew Hobbs and Durwyn Liley for information. Carlos thanks Aurélien Audevard and Daniele Occhiato for their generous photographic contributions, and Ana Bocos, Mario Tovar and Rizka Adelia Maharani for their continual support.

PHOTO CREDITS

All the photographs in this book were taken by Carlos Bocos, with the exception of the following: Alick Simmons: 16TL; Aurélien Audevard: 10TR, 11BR, 19TL, 21TL, 41BR, 45T, 45BR, 60BL, 62TL, 63CR2, 70T, 70B, 88CL, 88BL; Daniele Occhiato: 20T, 20B, 34TL, 34TR, 40B, 54T, 71B, 72T, 116TL, 127BL; James Lowen: 10BR, 11TL, 11TR, 14BL, 18BR, 39BR, 53BR, 58TL, 59CR, 60BR, 63CR1, 72BL, 83BR, 84TR, 84BL, 85TR, 87BL, 116TR, 122BR, 123TR, 127TL, 127TR, 127BR, 129TR; Jose Luis Rodriguez: 23TR, 27TR, 35B, 37TR, 38T, 69BR, 76TR, 85CR, 97BR, 122TR; Richard Bonser: 16TR.

LIST OF SPECIES NAMES

This list presents three names for each of the species described in this guide. The English name is indicated in upper case, the Spanish name in plain text and the scientific name in italics. With very occasional deviations, English and scientific names follow the taxonomy and nomenclature of the Association of European Records and Rarities Committees (www.aerc.eu), and Spanish names follow de Juana and Varela (2017). For Galician, Basque and Catalan names, see de Juana and Varela (2017).

English	Spanish	Scientific
GREYLAG GOOSE	Ánsar común	*Anser anser*
COMMON SHELDUCK	Tarro blanco	*Tadorna tadorna*
MALLARD	Ánade azulón	*Anas platyrhynchos*
EURASIAN WIGEON	Sibilón europeo	*Anas penelope*
GADWALL	Ánade friso	*Anas strepera*
EURASIAN TEAL	Cerceta común	*Anas crecca*
NORTHERN PINTAIL	Ánade rabudo	*Anas acuta*
GARGANEY	Cerceta carretona	*Anas querquedula*
NORTHERN SHOVELER	Cuchara común	*Anas clypeata*
RED-CRESTED POCHARD	Pato colorado	*Netta rufina*
COMMON POCHARD	Porrón europeo	*Aythya ferina*
TUFTED DUCK	Porrón moñudo	*Aythya fuligula*
COMMON SCOTER	Negrón común	*Melanitta nigra*
WHITE-HEADED DUCK	Malvasia cabeciblanca	*Oxyura leucocephala*
COMMON QUAIL	Codorniz común	*Coturnix coturnix*
RED-LEGGED PARTRIDGE	Perdiz roja	*Alectoris rufa*
GREAT NORTHERN DIVER	Colimbo grande	*Gavia immer*
LITTLE GREBE	Zampullín común	*Tachybaptus ruficollis*
GREAT CRESTED GREBE	Somormujo lavanco	*Podiceps cristatus*
BLACK-NECKED GREBE	Zampullín cuellinegro	*Podiceps nigricollis*
CORY'S SHEARWATER	Pardela cenicenta	*Calonectris diomedea*
BALEARIC SHEARWATER	Pardela balear	*Puffinus mauretanicus*
NORTHERN GANNET	Alcatraz atlántico	*Morus bassanus*
GREAT CORMORANT	Cormorán grande	*Phalacrocorax carbo*
EUROPEAN SHAG	Cormorán moñudo	*Phalacrocorax aristotelis*
LITTLE BITTERN	Avetorillo común	*Ixobrychus minutus*
BLACK-CROWNED NIGHT HERON	Martinete común	*Nycticorax nycticorax*
SQUACCO HERON	Garcilla cangrejera	*Ardeola ralloides*
CATTLE EGRET	Garcilla bueyera	*Bubulcus ibis*
LITTLE EGRET	Garcetta común	*Egretta garzetta*
GREAT EGRET	Garceta grande	*Egretta alba*
GREY HERON	Garza real	*Ardea cinerea*
PURPLE HERON	Garza imperial	*Ardea purpurea*
BLACK STORK	Cigüeña negra	*Ciconia nigra*
WHITE STORK	Cigüeña blanca	*Ciconia ciconia*
GLOSSY IBIS	Ibis eremita	*Plegadis falcinellus*
EURASIAN SPOONBILL	Espátula común	*Platalea leucorodia*
GREATER FLAMINGO	Flamenco común	*Phoenicopterus roseus*
EUROPEAN HONEY BUZZARD	Abejero europeo	*Pernis apivorus*
BLACK-WINGED KITE	Elanio común	*Elanus caeruleus*
BLACK KITE	Milano negro	*Milvus migrans*
RED KITE	Milano real	*Milvus milvus*
BEARDED VULTURE	Quebrantahuesos	*Gypaetus barbatus*
EGYPTIAN VULTURE	Alimoche común	*Neophron percnopterus*

GRIFFON VULTURE	Buitre leonardo	*Gyps fulvus*
CINEREOUS VULTURE	Buitre negro	*Aegypius monachus*
SHORT-TOED SNAKE EAGLE	Culebrera europea	*Circaetus gallicus*
WESTERN MARSH HARRIER	Aguilucho lagunero occidental	*Circus aeruginosus*
HEN HARRIER	Aguilucho pálido	*Circus cyaneus*
MONTAGU'S HARRIER	Aguilucho cenizo	*Circus pygargus*
NORTHERN GOSHAWK	Azor común	*Accipiter gentilis*
EURASIAN SPARROWHAWK	Gavilán común	*Accipiter nisus*
COMMON BUZZARD	Busardo ratonero	*Buteo buteo*
SPANISH IMPERIAL EAGLE	Águila imperial ibérica	*Aquila adalberti*
GOLDEN EAGLE	Águila real	*Aquila chrysaetos*
BOOTED EAGLE	Águila calzada	*Aquila pennata*
BONELLI'S EAGLE	Águila perdicera	*Aquila fasciata*
LESSER KESTREL	Cernícalo vulgar	*Falco naumanni*
COMMON KESTREL	Cernícalo común	*Falco tinnunculus*
EURASIAN HOBBY	Alcotán europeo	*Falco subbuteo*
ELEONORA'S FALCON	Halcón de Eleonora	*Falco eleonorae*
PEREGRINE FALCON	Halcón peregrino	*Falco peregrinus*
WATER RAIL	Rascón europeo	*Rallus aquaticus*
COMMON MOORHEN	Galineta común	*Gallinula chloropus*
PURPLE SWAMPHEN	Calamón común	*Porphyrio porphyrio*
EURASIAN COOT	Focha común	*Fulica atra*
COMMON CRANE	Grulla común	*Grus grus*
LITTLE BUSTARD	Sisón común	*Tetrax tetrax*
GREAT BUSTARD	Avutarda común	*Otis tarda*
EURASIAN STONE-CURLEW	Alcaraván común	*Burhinus oedicnemus*
BLACK-WINGED STILT	Cigüenela común	*Himantopus himantopus*
PIED AVOCET	Avoceta común	*Recurvirostra avosetta*
EURASIAN OYSTERCATCHER	Ostrero euroasiático	*Haematopus ostralegus*
COLLARED PRATINCOLE	Canastera común	*Glareola pratincola*
EUROPEAN GOLDEN PLOVER	Chorlito dorado europeo	*Pluvialis apricaria*
GREY PLOVER	Chorlito gris	*Pluvialis squatarola*
NORTHERN LAPWING	Avefría europea	*Vanellus vanellus*
LITTLE RINGED PLOVER	Chorlitejo chico	*Charadrius dubius*
COMMON RINGED PLOVER	Chorlitejo grande	*Charadrius hiaticula*
KENTISH PLOVER	Chorlitejo patinegro	*Charadrius alexandrinus*
WHIMBREL	Zarapito trinador	*Numenius phaeopus*
EURASIAN CURLEW	Zarapito real	*Numenius arquata*
BLACK-TAILED GODWIT	Aguja colinegra	*Limosa limosa*
RUDDY TURNSTONE	Vuelvepiedras común	*Arenaria interpres*
SANDERLING	Correlimos tridáctilo	*Calidris alba*
DUNLIN	Correlimos común	*Calidris alpina*
LITTLE STINT	Correlimos menudo	*Calidris minuta*
RUFF	Combatiente	*Calidris pugnax*
EURASIAN WOODCOCK	Chocha perdiz	*Scolopax rusticola*
COMMON SNIPE	Agachadiza común	*Gallinago gallinago*
COMMON SANDPIPER	Andarríos chico	*Actitis hypoleucos*
GREEN SANDPIPER	Andarríos grande	*Tringa ochropus*
SPOTTED REDSHANK	Archibebe oscuro	*Tringa erythropus*
COMMON GREENSHANK	Archibebe claro	*Tringa nebularia*
WOOD SANDPIPER	Andarríos bastardo	*Tringa glareola*
COMMON REDSHANK	Archibebe común	*Tringa totanus*

LITTLE TERN	Charrancito común	*Sternula albifrons*
GULL-BILLED TERN	Pagaza piconegra	*Gelochelidon nilotica*
WHISKERED TERN	Furnarel común	*Chlidonias hybrida*
SANDWICH TERN	Charrán patinegro	*Sterna sandvicensis*
COMMON TERN	Charrán común	*Sterna hirundo*
BLACK-LEGGED KITTIWAKE	Gaviota tridáctila	*Rissa tridactyla*
SLENDER-BILLED GULL	Gaviota picofina	*Larus genei*
BLACK-HEADED GULL	Gaviota reidora	*Larus ridibundus*
MEDITERRANEAN GULL	Gaviota cabecinegra	*Larus melanocephalus*
AUDOUIN'S GULL	Gaviota de Audouin	*Larus audouinii*
LESSER BLACK-BACKED GULL	Gaviota sombría	*Larus fuscus*
EUROPEAN HERRING GULL	Gaviota argéntea europea	*Larus argentatus*
YELLOW-LEGGED GULL	Gaviota patiamarilla	*Larus michahellis*
BLACK-BELLIED SANDGROUSE	Ganga ortega	*Pterocles orientalis*
PIN-TAILED SANDGROUSE	Ganga ibérica	*Pterocles alchata*
ROCK DOVE/FERAL PIGEON	Paloma bravía	*Columba livia*
STOCK DOVE	Paloma zurita	*Columba oenas*
COMMON WOOD PIGEON	Paloma torcaz	*Columba palumbus*
EURASIAN COLLARED DOVE	Tórtola turca	*Streptopelia decaocto*
EUROPEAN TURTLE DOVE	Tórtola europea	*Streptopelia turtur*
MONK PARAKEET	Cotorra argentina	*Myiopsitta monachus*
GREAT SPOTTED CUCKOO	Crialo europeo	*Clamator glandarius*
COMMON CUCKOO	Cuco común	*Cuculus canorus*
BARN OWL	Lechuza común	*Tyto alba*
EURASIAN SCOPS OWL	Autillo europeo	*Otus scops*
EURASIAN EAGLE-OWL	Búho real	*Bubo bubo*
LITTLE OWL	Mochuelo europeo	*Athene noctua*
TAWNY OWL	Cárabo común	*Strix aluco*
LONG-EARED OWL	Búho chico	*Asio otus*
SHORT-EARED OWL	Búho campestre	*Asio flammeus*
EUROPEAN NIGHTJAR	Chotacabras europeo	*Caprimulgus europaeus*
RED-NECKED NIGHTJAR	Chotacabras cuellirrojo	*Caprimulgus ruficollis*
COMMON SWIFT	Vencejo común	*Apus apus*
PALLID SWIFT	Vencejo pálido	*Apus pallidus*
ALPINE SWIFT	Vencejo real	*Apus melba*
COMMON KINGFISHER	Martín pescador común	*Alcedo atthis*
EUROPEAN BEE-EATER	Abejaruco europeo	*Merops apiaster*
EUROPEAN ROLLER	Carraca europea	*Coracias garrulus*
HOOPOE	Abubilla común	*Upupa epops*
EURASIAN WRYNECK	Torsecuello euroasiático	*Jynx torquilla*
EUROPEAN GREEN WOODPECKER	Pito real ibérico	*Picus viridis*
GREAT SPOTTED WOODPECKER	Pico picapinos	*Dendrocopos major*
MIDDLE SPOTTED WOODPECKER	Pico mediano	*Dendrocopos medius*
DUPONT'S LARK	Arlondra ricotí	*Chersophilus duponti*
CALANDRA LARK	Calandria común	*Melanocorypha calandra*
GREATER SHORT-TOED LARK	Terrera común	*Calandrella brachydactyla*
LESSER SHORT-TOED LARK	Terrera marismeña	*Calandrella rufescens*
CRESTED LARK	Cogujada común	*Galerida cristata*
THEKLA LARK	Cogujada montesina	*Galerida theklae*
WOODLARK	Arlondra totovía	*Lullula arborea*
EURASIAN SKYLARK	Arlondra común	*Alauda arvensis*
SAND MARTIN	Avión zapador	*Riparia riparia*

EURASIAN CRAG MARTIN	Avión roquero	*Ptyonoprogne rupestris*
BARN SWALLOW	Golondrina común	*Hirundo rustica*
COMMON HOUSE MARTIN	Avión común	*Delichon urbicum*
RED-RUMPED SWALLOW	Golondrina dáurica	*Cecropis daurica*
TAWNY PIPIT	Bisbita campestre	*Anthus campestris*
TREE PIPIT	Bisbita arbóreo	*Anthus trivialis*
MEADOW PIPIT	Bisbita pratense	*Anthus pratensis*
WATER PIPIT	Bisbita alpino	*Anthus spinoletta*
GREY WAGTAIL	Lavandera cascadeña	*Motacilla cinerea*
YELLOW WAGTAIL	Lavandera boyera	*Motacilla flava*
WHITE WAGTAIL	Lavandera blanca	*Motacilla alba*
WHITE-THROATED DIPPER	Mirlo acuático europeo	*Cinclus cinclus*
WINTER WREN	Chochín común	*Troglodytes troglodytes*
DUNNOCK	Acentor común	*Prunella modularis*
ALPINE ACCENTOR	Acentor alpino	*Prunella collaris*
RUFOUS-TAILED SCRUB ROBIN	Alza cola rojizo	*Cercotrichas galactotes*
EUROPEAN ROBIN	Petirrojo europeo	*Erithacus rubecula*
COMMON NIGHTINGALE	Ruiseñor común	*Luscinia megarhynchos*
BLUETHROAT	Ruiseñor pechiazul	*Luscinia svecica*
BLACK REDSTART	Colirrojo tizón	*Phoenicurus ochruros*
COMMON REDSTART	Colirrojo real	*Phoenicurus phoenicurus*
WHINCHAT	Tarabilla norteña	*Saxicola rubetra*
EUROPEAN STONECHAT	Tarabilla común	*Saxicola rubicola*
NORTHERN WHEATEAR	Collalba gris	*Oenanthe oenanthe*
BLACK-EARED WHEATEAR	Collalba rubia	*Oenanthe hispanica*
BLACK WHEATEAR	Collalba negra	*Oenanthe leucura*
COMMON ROCK THRUSH	Roquero rojo	*Monticola saxatilis*
BLUE ROCK THRUSH	Roquero solitario	*Monticola solitarius*
RING OUZEL	Mirlo capiblanco	*Turdus torquatus*
COMMON BLACKBIRD	Mirlo común	*Turdus merula*
SONG THRUSH	Zorzal común	*Turdus philomelos*
REDWING	Zorzal alirrojo	*Turdus iliacus*
MISTLE THRUSH	Zorzal charlo	*Turdus viscivorus*
CETTI'S WARBLER	Cetia ruiseñor	*Cettia cetti*
ZITTING CISTICOLA	Cisticola buitrón	*Cisticola juncidis*
COMMON GRASSHOPPER WARBLER	Buscarla pintoja	*Locustella naevia*
WESTERN OLIVACEOUS WARBLER	Zarcero bereber	*Iduna opaca*
MELODIOUS WARBLER	Zarcero común	*Hippolais polyglotta*
EURASIAN REED WARBLER	Carricero común	*Acrocephalus scirpaceus*
GREAT REED WARBLER	Carricero tordal	*Acrocephalus arundinaceus*
BALEARIC WARBLER	Curruca balear	*Sylvia balearica*
DARTFORD WARBLER	Curruca rabilarga	*Sylvia undata*
SPECTACLED WARBLER	Curruca tomillera	*Sylvia conspicillata*
SUBALPINE WARBLER	Curruca carrasqueña	*Sylvia cantillans*
SARDINIAN WARBLER	Curruca cabecinegra	*Sylvia melanocephala*
WESTERN ORPHEAN WARBLER	Curruca mirlona	*Sylvia hortensis*
COMMON WHITETHROAT	Curruca communis	*Sylvia communis*
GARDEN WARBLER	Curruca mosquitera	*Sylvia borin*
EURASIAN BLACKCAP	Curruca capirotada	*Sylvia atricapilla*
WESTERN BONELLI'S WARBLER	Mosquitero papialbo	*Phylloscopus bonelli*
COMMON CHIFFCHAFF	Mosquitero común	*Phylloscopus collybita*
IBERIAN CHIFFCHAFF	Mosquitero ibérico	*Phylloscopus ibericus*

WILLOW WARBLER	Mosquitero musical	*Phylloscopus trochilus*
GOLDCREST	Reyezuelo sencillo	*Regulus regulus*
COMMON FIRECREST	Reyezuelo listado	*Regulus ignicapilla*
SPOTTED FLYCATCHER	Papamoscas gris	*Muscicapa striata*
EUROPEAN PIED FLYCATCHER	Papamoscas cerrojillo	*Ficedula hypoleuca*
LONG-TAILED TIT	Mito común	*Aegithalos caudatus*
MARSH TIT	Carbonero palustre	*Poecile palustris*
EUROPEAN CRESTED TIT	Herrerillo capuchino europeo	*Lophophranes cristatus*
COAL TIT	Carbonero garrapinos	*Periparus ater*
EURASIAN BLUE TIT	Herrerillo común	*Cyanistes caeruleus*
GREAT TIT	Carbonero común	*Parus major*
EURASIAN NUTHATCH	Trepador azul	*Sitta europaea*
WALLCREEPER	Treparriscos	*Tichodroma muraria*
SHORT-TOED TREECREEPER	Agateador europeo	*Certhia brachydactyla*
EURASIAN PENDULINE TIT	Pájaro moscón europeo	*Remiz pendulinus*
EURASIAN GOLDEN ORIOLE	Oropéndula europea	*Oriolus oriolus*
RED-BACKED SHRIKE	Alcaudón dorsirrojo	*Lanius collurio*
SOUTHERN GREY SHRIKE	Alcaudón real	*Lanius meridionalis*
WOODCHAT SHRIKE	Alcaudón común	*Lanius senator*
EURASIAN JAY	Arrendajo euroasiático	*Garrulus glandarius*
AZURE-WINGED MAGPIE	Rabilargo ibérico	*Cyanopica cyanus*
COMMON MAGPIE	Urraca común	*Pica pica*
ALPINE CHOUGH	Chova piquigualda	*Pyrrhocorax graculus*
RED-BILLED CHOUGH	Chova piquirroja	*Pyrrhocorax pyrrhocorax*
WESTERN JACKDAW	Grajilla occidental	*Corvus monedula*
CARRION CROW	Corneja negra	*Corvus corone*
NORTHERN RAVEN	Cuervo grande	*Corvus corax*
SPOTLESS STARLING	Estornino negro	*Sturnus unicolor*
COMMON STARLING	Estornino pinto	*Sturnus vulgaris*
HOUSE SPARROW	Gorrión común	*Passer domesticus*
SPANISH SPARROW	Gorrión moruno	*Passer hispaniolensis*
EURASIAN TREE SPARROW	Gorrión molinero	*Passer montanus*
ROCK SPARROW	Gorrión chillón	*Petronia petronia*
WHITE-WINGED SNOWFINCH	Gorrión alpino	*Montifringilla nivalis*
COMMON WAXBILL	Estrilda común	*Estrilda astrild*
RED AVADAVAT	Bengalí rojo	*Amandava amandava*
COMMON CHAFFINCH	Pinzón vulgar	*Fringilla coelebs*
EUROPEAN SERIN	Serín verdecillo	*Serinus serinus*
CITRIL FINCH	Verderón serrano	*Serinus citrinella*
EUROPEAN GREENFINCH	Verderón común	*Carduelis chloris*
EUROPEAN GOLDFINCH	Jilguero europeo	*Carduelis carduelis*
EURASIAN SISKIN	Jilguero lúgano	*Carduelis spinus*
COMMON LINNET	Pardillo común	*Carduelis cannabina*
RED CROSSBILL	Piquituerto común	*Loxia curvirostra*
EURASIAN BULLFINCH	Camachuelo común	*Pyrrhula pyrrhula*
HAWFINCH	Picogordo común	*Coccothraustes coccothraustes*
YELLOWHAMMER	Escribano cerillo	*Emberiza citrinella*
CIRL BUNTING	Escribano soteño	*Emberiza cirlus*
ROCK BUNTING	Escribano montesino	*Emberiza cia*
ORTOLAN BUNTING	Escribano hortelano	*Emberiza hortulana*
COMMON REED BUNTING	Escribano palustre	*Emberiza schoeniclus*
CORN BUNTING	Escribano triguero	*Emberiza calandra*

INDEX